First Job Jitters

A Buffoon's Guide to Full-Time Work!

Join the uproarious misadventures of a bumbling protagonist as they navigate their first full-time job, a hilarious journey filled with resume blunders, office pranks, and an eccentric cast of co-workers, all wrapped in classic British humour.

Contents

The Dreaded Interview Dance

As I stood outside the imposing glass doors of "Dream Inc." – my tie askew and heart pounding like a herd of stampeding wildebeests – I couldn't help but question why on earth I had decided to wear my older brother's oversized suit for the big interview. It seemed that "dressing for success" had turned me into a lanky penguin waddling down the pavement.

Finally, I mustered the courage to enter the sleek, modern building. The receptionist, impeccably groomed and poised, greeted me with a warm smile that only made my nerves jangle louder. She asked me to take a seat and wait for Mr. Thompson, the HR manager.

Sitting in that elegantly designed waiting area, I couldn't help but notice the other candidates. All of them seemed so put-together, like they had stepped out of a magazine cover for "Job Seekers Monthly." Meanwhile, I was there, an anxious mess with a résumé that probably looked like a child's attempt at writing a wish list to Santa.

When Mr. Thompson finally emerged from his office, I tried to stand up confidently, but my foot caught in the carpet, and I stumbled forward, barely catching myself from face-planting into the floor. I could have sworn I saw the receptionist's eyes widen in surprise, but she maintained her composure with admirable professionalism.

"Mr. Smith?" Mr. Thompson extended his hand, and I managed to shake it without further humiliation.

"Yes, that's me," I replied, my voice cracking like a pre-pubescent teenager.

We entered his office, and I sat down, trying my best not to fidget in the giant chair that seemed designed to swallow me whole. As Mr. Thompson glanced at my résumé, I braced myself for the first question.

"So, tell me about yourself," he said, leaning back in his chair.

And there it was, the most dreaded and open-ended question that could make any interviewee's mind go completely blank. I cleared my throat and began my well-rehearsed answer, but all that came out was a string of incoherent words and awkward giggles. I might have even thrown in a snort somewhere, though I hoped he didn't notice.

I could see the concern in his eyes as he tried to decipher what on earth was happening before him. "Nerves," I muttered, my cheeks turning crimson.

"No worries," he said with a kind smile. "It happens to the best of us. Let's move on to your previous work experience."

Relieved to have survived the "tell me about yourself" ordeal, I dove into my previous jobs, exaggerating my accomplishments to appear more impressive than I probably was. He nodded politely, occasionally scribbling something on a notepad.

Then, he leaned forward, steepling his fingers. "Can you give me an example of how you handle stressful situations?"

I recalled a time when I had to handle an irate customer at my part-time job in a fast-food restaurant. However, the moment I started telling the story, I found myself unintentionally reenacting the scene, complete with wild hand gestures and different voices for each character.

I must have looked like a one-man theatre performance, and when I finished, I half-expected Mr. Thompson to give me a standing ovation. Instead, he blinked a couple of times and asked, "Well, that's quite a vivid description, Mr. Smith. But how do you manage stress in a professional setting?"

Flustered, I mumbled something about taking deep breaths and counting to ten but managed to throw in a pirate impression midway through. I don't think pirates were exactly known for their stress-management techniques, but there it was.

Mr. Thompson's facial expression remained impressively neutral as he continued with the interview. It seemed like he was determined to finish this dance, no matter how awkwardly I stumbled through it.

Finally, we reached the end of the interview, and he asked if I had any questions. I had prepared a few intelligent-sounding inquiries, but in my frazzled state, all I could think of was asking if the office had a designated snack area. He politely assured me that they did, though I suspected my chances of landing the job were now as slim as fitting into my younger brother's shoes.

As I left the interview, I couldn't help but laugh at the absurdity of it all. The dreaded interview dance had been a hilarious spectacle, and though my chances of getting the job might have been slim, I knew one thing for sure – I had certainly left an impression, whether good or bad, remained to be seen.

When My Resume Became a Work of Fiction

I had always been told that honesty is the best policy, especially when it came to job applications. But after months of rejections and no calls for interviews, I started to wonder if my truthfulness was the reason for my lack of success. Perhaps it was time to take a more creative approach.

One fateful evening, fuelled by a potent combination of desperation and a glass of cheap wine, I decided to give my resume a makeover. I turned on my laptop, opened Microsoft Word, and stared at the blank page. The cursor blinked expectantly, mocking me for my lack of imagination.

I began with the basics: my name, contact information, and education. But as I moved on to my work experience, I felt a surge of inspiration. Instead of the mundane tasks I had performed at my previous jobs, I transformed them into feats of heroism and daring.

Under "Customer Service Representative," I wrote: "Successfully resolved a hostile takeover attempt by a disgruntled customer, saving the company from certain doom." I couldn't help but chuckle at the audacity of my embellishment.

Next came my part-time job as a cashier, which I transformed into: "Master of quick calculations, accurately computing change in a matter of seconds, while foiling numerous attempts at counterfeit bill circulation." Surely, employers would be lining up to hire such a skilled and vigilant cashier!

I decided to go all out with my retail experience, embellishing my role as a sales associate: "Single-handedly increased store sales by 200% through an expert use of persuasive charm and Jedi mind tricks." I smirked, imagining myself waving my hand and saying, "These are the products you're looking for."

Feeling like a literary genius, I moved on to my skills section. Instead of listing the standard skills like "Microsoft Office proficiency," I proudly declared: "Possesses a magical touch with technology, effortlessly conjuring up solutions to any IT problem with a wave of a wand... uh, mouse."

I hesitated for a moment, questioning my sanity, but then decided to go all-in with my newfound creativity. I added "Fluent in five languages," which was technically true, if you counted Pig Latin, Simlish (the language from The Sims game), and the gibberish my siblings and I made up as languages.

As I read over my revamped resume, I couldn't help but snicker at the absurdity of it all. It was as if I had turned my professional life into a fantasy novel, where I was the hero with magical abilities and incredible achievements. But deep down, I knew this was all just a humorous ploy, a way to inject some fun into the dreary job search.

With a mix of amusement and anxiety, I started sending out my newly crafted masterpiece to potential employers. As the days passed, the silence was deafening. Had my creative writing skills scared them away? Or were they simply not ready to appreciate the brilliance of my imaginative storytelling?

Just when I was about to throw in the towel and go back to my honest but seemingly unimpressive resume, I received an email from a prestigious company. They wanted to schedule an interview! My heart leaped with excitement, and for a moment, I considered wearing a cape and carrying a wand to the interview just to see their reaction.

But as the interview day approached, my nerves started to get the better of me. What if they asked me about my magical achievements, and I couldn't keep up the act? What if they saw through my facade and realized I was just an ordinary job seeker with an extraordinary imagination?

In the end, I decided to come clean. As I sat across from the interviewer, I took a deep breath and confessed that my resume was a playful exaggeration, a work of fiction born out of desperation and a desire to stand out.

To my surprise, the interviewer burst into laughter. "I have to say, your resume is one of the most entertaining ones we've ever received," he said with a grin. "We could all use a bit of magic in our lives, especially in the workplace."

As it turned out, my creative resume had done the unexpected – it had set me apart from the sea of other applicants and made me memorable in the best possible way. The company appreciated the humour and the willingness to take risks, qualities they believed would be an asset in their team.

In the end, I got the job – not because of my fictional achievements, but because of my willingness to think outside the box and inject some much-needed humour into the serious world of job hunting. It was a lesson that sometimes, being yourself and showing a little creativity can open doors that a standard resume never could.

And so, I learned that while honesty is undoubtedly crucial, a sprinkle of creativity and humour can turn a mundane job search into an unforgettable adventure. From that day forward, I vowed to bring a touch of magic into every aspect of my professional life, proving that sometimes, a bit of fiction can make reality just a little bit more enchanting.

Dressing for Success
(Or So I Thought)

They say that first impressions are everything, especially in the world of job interviews. Armed with this sage advice, I embarked on my quest to find the perfect outfit that would exude confidence, professionalism, and undeniable charm. Little did I know that my idea of "dressing for success" would take a detour into the realm of hilarity.

I rummaged through my closet, searching for the ideal ensemble that would scream "hire me!" Amidst the sea of t-shirts and worn-out jeans, I found a dusty old suit that had not seen the light of day in years. It was a bit snug around the waist, but I figured it was a sign to hit the gym – what better motivation than a job interview?

With the suit in hand, I headed to the mirror to admire my transformation into a suave and sophisticated professional. Instead, I saw a scrawny fellow who seemed to have borrowed his father's clothes for a fancy dress party. But I wasn't going to let a minor detail like fit deter me from my mission.

Next on the list was the tie – a quintessential symbol of professionalism. I reached into the abyss of my drawer and pulled out a tie with a flamboyant pattern of neon flamingos. It had been a gag gift from a friend, but it seemed like a fun way to add a touch of personality to my otherwise conservative attire.

Once I had donned the suit and tie, I stood before the mirror, practicing my firm handshake and confident smile. The result was more akin to a teenager playing dress-up than a serious job applicant. But I was determined to make it work. "Fake it till you make it," they said.

The morning of the interview arrived, and I set off with an air of self-assuredness that didn't quite match the butterflies doing acrobatics in my stomach. As I walked down the street, I received a few quizzical glances, which I chose to interpret as admiration for my bold fashion statement.

With my chin held high, I entered the imposing building that housed my potential employer. The receptionist gave me a polite smile, though her eyes seemed to linger on the flamboyant flamingos. Nevertheless, I pressed on, reminding myself that confidence was the key.

As I waited for my turn, I noticed the other candidates around me, all dressed in the standard corporate attire. Their suits were impeccable, their ties tasteful — they looked like they had walked straight out of a boardroom meeting. Meanwhile, I stood there like an exotic bird in a sea of penguins.

When it was finally my turn, I entered the interview room, determined to make a lasting impression. But the moment I extended my hand for a handshake, I noticed the interviewer's eyebrows shoot up in surprise. I mentally cringed as I realized he was probably trying to figure out whether I was serious or the subject of a hidden camera show.

Nevertheless, I forged ahead, answering questions with what I hoped was a winning combination of charm and professionalism. But every time I caught a glimpse of the neon flamingos peeking out from my suit, I had to suppress a giggle.

The interviewer's poker face was impressive, revealing nothing about his thoughts on my fashion choices. However, when he finally asked about my suitability for the position, I felt it was time to address the sartorial elephant in the room.

"Well," I began, flashing what I hoped was a disarming smile, "I believe in standing out from the crowd, and I thought the flamingos would do the trick."

To my surprise, the interviewer's stern expression broke into a smile. "You certainly did stand out," he said, trying to hide a chuckle.

I took a deep breath, deciding to embrace the absurdity of the situation. "In all seriousness," I continued, "I believe that a bit of personality can go a long way, even in a professional setting."

To my amazement, the interviewer nodded thoughtfully. "You have a point there," he said, "and I must say, you've left a lasting impression."

I left the interview feeling a mix of relief and amusement. While my fashion choices might have raised a few eyebrows, I had managed to turn what could have been a disastrous interview into a memorable one.

As I walked back home, I pondered the lesson I had learned that day. Perhaps "dressing for success" wasn't about conforming to the conventional norms but about showcasing who you truly were, even if that meant donning a tie with neon flamingos.

In the end, I didn't get the job, but I did receive something invaluable – a newfound sense of authenticity. From that day forward, I vowed to embrace my quirks and let my personality shine through, even in the most formal of settings.

So, the next time I had an interview, I traded the stuffy suit for a more comfortable but polished outfit that still carried a hint of my unique style. I may not have landed the job that time either, but I knew that my authenticity had brought me one step closer to finding the perfect fit – both in terms of a career and a wardrobe. And who knows, maybe one day, a company will see the value in hiring a candidate who isn't afraid to stand out from the crowd, flamingos and all.

The Unintentional Hilarities of My Cover Letter

Ah, the cover letter – that dreaded piece of professional literature designed to showcase one's skills, experience, and professionalism. Little did I know that my attempt at writing a stellar cover letter would turn into a comedic masterpiece, unintentionally filled with hilarities that would leave recruiters laughing for days.

With determination and a steaming cup of coffee by my side, I sat down at my laptop, ready to craft the ultimate cover letter that would set me apart from the competition. Armed with a thesaurus and an air of self-assuredness, I began typing away, determined to make my words leap off the page like a Broadway performance.

Dear Hiring Manager,

I hope this letter finds you in the best of health and humour. As a seasoned professional with a proven track record of exceptional achievements, I am thrilled to submit my application for the [insert job title here] position at [insert company name here].

Off to a good start, or so I thought. I read over my opening sentence with a sense of satisfaction, imagining the hiring manager nodding in approval at my eloquent prose. But little did I know that my next sentence would take a comedic turn of its own.

Throughout my career, I have demonstrated a keen eye for detail and a knack for turning complex challenges into golden opportunities. My colleagues often describe me as the "Sherlock Holmes of problem-solving," always one step ahead of the game.

I paused for a moment, contemplating the image of myself in a deerstalker cap and a magnifying glass, wandering around the office like a detective on the case. The mental image was far from professional, but it did bring a smile to my face.

In my desire to impress, I decided to delve into the world of business jargon, hoping to dazzle the reader with my knowledge of buzzwords and corporate lingo.

I am well-versed in synergizing cross-functional teams and leveraging core competencies to drive bottom-line results. With a growth mindset and a passion for disruption, I am confident that my skills align perfectly with the vision and mission of [insert company name here].

Feeling quite pleased with myself, I imagined the hiring manager reading my cover letter with awe, marvelling at my mastery of business-speak. However, I couldn't help but chuckle at the thought of "synergizing cross-functional teams" and "passion for disruption" – it sounded like something out of a corporate buzzword bingo game.

As I continued writing, I decided to throw in a dash of humility, lest I come across as too self-assured.

While my achievements have been nothing short of awe-inspiring, I humbly acknowledge that there is always room for growth and improvement. I am committed to continuous learning and development, always seeking to expand my horizons and level up my skillset.

Ah, yes, my "awe-inspiring" achievements, indeed! I couldn't help but imagine the recruiter rolling their eyes at my attempt to downplay my accomplishments with such grandiose language.

As I reached the end of my cover letter, I wanted to leave a lasting impression that would be etched into the hiring manager's memory forever.

In conclusion, I am more than just a qualified candidate – I am a force of nature, a typhoon of talent, ready to sweep through [insert company name here] and leave a trail of success in my wake. I eagerly await the opportunity to discuss in person how I can contribute to the continued greatness of your esteemed organization.

Typhoon of talent? Surely, I had taken my enthusiasm a tad too far. I imagined myself storming into the office for the interview, complete with sound effects of thunder and lightning. It was a humorous mental image, but one that probably wouldn't land me the job.

Feeling a mix of amusement and slight embarrassment, I proofread my cover letter one last time before hitting the send button. Part of me wanted to delete the over-the-top statements and replace them with more standard fare, but another part of me appreciated the comedic charm that had unintentionally infused my letter.

As I sent off my cover letter into the digital abyss, I couldn't help but wonder how it would be received on the other end. Would the hiring manager see through the unintentional hilarities and appreciate the quirky personality behind the words? Or would they dismiss me as a candidate who didn't take the application process seriously?

In the end, I may never know the true impact of my cover letter, but one thing was for sure – it had provided me with a good laugh and a reminder that sometimes, authenticity and humour can shine through, even in the most professional of settings. And if nothing else, it was a great story to tell at parties – the tale of the cover letter that unintentionally became a comedic gem.

Commuting Chaos

Navigating the Public Transport Circus

Ah, the daily commute – a wondrous adventure through the wild jungles of public transportation. Little did I know that my journey to work each day would be a hilariously chaotic circus act, complete with unexpected surprises, zany characters, and daring feats of balance.

The first act of the circus began at the bus stop, where a diverse cast of characters gathered each morning. There was the "Overenthusiastic Early Bird," always the first to arrive, bouncing with energy as if they had just downed a gallon of coffee. Then there was the "Disgruntled Commuter," who grumbled and sighed at every minor inconvenience, from a slight drizzle to a momentary delay.

One morning, I found myself standing next to the "Chatterbox Traveler," a person who seemed determined to engage everyone in a conversation about their life story. As they prattled on about their cats and their latest vacation, I nodded politely while desperately hoping for the bus to arrive and whisk me away from the chatter.

Finally, the bus arrived, and the real circus began. As the doors opened, there was a mad dash for the limited number of seats. It was every commuter for themselves, and I found myself caught in a battle of wills with a fellow passenger who was equally determined to secure the last available seat. In the end, we both lunged for it simultaneously, only to end up sitting awkwardly half on the seat and half on each other's laps.

Once settled in my precarious perch, the bus embarked on a bumpy journey that felt like a rollercoaster ride. I clung to the handrails for dear life, praying that I wouldn't be launched into the air with every sharp turn. The driver seemed to be channelling their inner stunt driver, weaving in and out of traffic with a daredevil's flair.

As if that wasn't enough, the onboard entertainment added another layer of absurdity to the circus. The "Accidental DJ" commuter played music from their phone, seemingly oblivious to the fact that we were not, in fact, at a party. Their eclectic playlist ranged from classical symphonies to heavy metal, leaving the rest of us thoroughly entertained or exasperated, depending on our musical tastes.

Just when I thought the circus couldn't get any wilder, the bus stopped abruptly, and a street performer hopped on board. With a guitar in hand and a spark in their eye, they serenaded us with an impromptu rendition of a classic rock song. The entire bus turned into a makeshift concert hall, with some passengers joining in on the chorus and others tapping their feet in rhythm.

The commute took a surreal turn when a magician boarded the bus. Decked out in a top hat and a cape, they proceeded to dazzle us with their tricks, making coins disappear and cards materialize out of thin air.

It was as if the bus had been transformed into a traveling circus, complete with its very own magician on board.

As the magician's act drew to a close, I couldn't help but marvel at the sheer randomness of the commute. Who would have thought that a simple bus ride could turn into a carnival of unexpected surprises and quirky performances?

At last, the bus arrived at my stop, and I bid farewell to my fellow circus-goers. Stepping out into the chaos of the city, I felt a mix of exhaustion and amusement. While the daily commute was undoubtedly chaotic, it was also a source of endless entertainment and camaraderie with fellow travellers.

But the circus wasn't over just yet. The next leg of my journey involved navigating the bustling subway system, a feat that required a delicate balance of grace and agility. I hopped onto the crowded train, sandwiched between commuters like a sardine in a can. As the train lurched forward, I clung to the overhead bar, my feet instinctively adjusting to the swaying rhythm of the subway.

As the train rattled along the tracks, I couldn't help but be amazed at the variety of characters that filled the carriage. There was the "Sleeping Beauty," nodding off with their head bobbing like a metronome. Then there was the "Workaholic Typist," furiously tapping away on their laptop, seemingly oblivious to the jostling of the train.

Of course, no subway ride would be complete without the "Sudden Dancer," who would break into an impromptu dance routine as if the train were their personal stage. I marvelled at their courage and enviable lack of self-consciousness, even as fellow commuters gave them amused glances.

Just when I thought I had seen it all, the doors of the subway opened to reveal a group of performers – acrobats, no less! They tumbled and flipped in the narrow aisle, narrowly avoiding kicking their fellow passengers in the face. It was an impressive display of talent and flexibility, but I couldn't help but worry about the safety hazards of acrobatics on a moving train.

As the subway reached my destination, I stepped off the train, bidding farewell to the circus that had been my daily commute. With a mix of relief and amusement, I realized that despite the chaos and absurdity, the journey had become a highlight of my day.

In the world of public transportation, every day was a new adventure, with unexpected surprises, eccentric characters, and a delightful dose of humour. It was a reminder that even in the midst of the daily grind, there was always room for a bit of fun and light-heartedness.

So, as I made my way to work, I embraced the commuting circus with a smile, eager to see what delightful performances and unexpected acts awaited me on the journey ahead. And as the bus rolled up, I stepped aboard with a sense of anticipation, ready for the next chapter of the hilariously chaotic circus that was my daily commute.

Coffee Mishaps and Other Office Accidents

In the office, coffee was more than just a beverage; it was the elixir of productivity, the lifeblood that fuelled our daily endeavours. But little did we know that our beloved coffee would become the catalyst for a series of hilarious mishaps and office accidents that would leave us in stitches.

It all began innocently enough, with a freshly brewed pot of coffee sitting temptingly on the communal kitchen counter. As the aroma wafted through the office, we all gravitated towards the source of this magical potion. But in our haste to get our caffeine fix, we failed to notice the ominous signs.

As I reached for the coffee pot, my clumsy fingers betrayed me, and the next thing I knew, a dark brown river was cascading down my shirt and tie. I was a walking coffee catastrophe, and my colleagues couldn't help but chuckle at my unfortunate mishap.

But I wasn't alone in my coffee calamity. Oh no, the office had its fair share of coffee spillers and mishap makers. There was the "Sloshing Sipper" who managed to spill coffee on themselves every morning, no matter how careful they were. Then there was the "Coffee Conductor," who somehow managed to knock over the coffee pot every time they passed by the kitchen counter.

But the pinnacle of coffee mishaps came one fateful day when a new intern joined the office. Eager to make a good impression, they decided to take on the responsibility of making a fresh pot of coffee for everyone. Little did they know that this innocent act of kindness would turn into an unforgettable office accident.

As the intern prepared the coffee, their enthusiasm got the best of them, and they accidentally poured coffee grounds directly into the coffee maker's water reservoir. It was a disaster waiting to happen, and happen it did.

The office erupted into chaos as the coffee maker sputtered and groaned, unable to handle the coffee grounds clogging its delicate inner workings. The poor intern watched in horror as the coffee maker transformed into a fuming, steaming mess, sending plumes of hot coffee grounds and water shooting out like a volcano.

It was a spectacle to behold – a coffee eruption of epic proportions. The office floor became a slip-and-slide of coffee grounds, and the air was filled with the aroma of freshly brewed coffee mixed with a hint of panic.

But amidst the chaos, there was no time to cry over spilled coffee. We had to act fast to prevent further disaster. In a moment of collective genius, someone grabbed a mop, and we all pitched in to clean up the mess. It was a team effort, with coffee grounds being scooped up like confetti after a party gone wild.

As the intern looked on, mortified and apologetic, we assured them that it was all part of the office initiation — a rite of passage, if you will. They may have unintentionally created a coffee catastrophe, but they had also earned their place in the annals of office history.

From that day forward, the intern became known as the "Coffee Groundbreaker," and their mishap became a legendary tale passed down from one batch of new employees to the next. They had unwittingly left their mark on the office, and their story would forever be etched into the coffee-stained fabric of our workplace lore.

But coffee mishaps were not the only office accidents that brought humour into our daily grind. Oh no, the office was a breeding ground for accidental hilarities of all kinds.

There was the "Printer Prankster," who innocently decided to pull a harmless prank by swapping the office printer's paper with a stack of neon-coloured paper. The result? A series of memos and reports that looked like they were straight out of a highlighter factory.

Then there was the "Keyboard Composer," who managed to accidentally change the settings of their computer keyboard to play musical notes with every keystroke. Their frantic typing sessions turned into impromptu piano recitals, much to the amusement of their neighbouring colleagues.

And let's not forget the "Chair Chameleon," who accidentally sat on a pen and managed to leave a trail of ink wherever they went. It was like a game of "spot the ink stain" as we discovered little blue surprises on chairs, desks, and even the floor.

But perhaps the most legendary of all office accidents was the "Elevator Escapade." It all started when the office elevator got stuck between floors, leaving a group of employees trapped inside. Panic ensued, but as the minutes turned into hours, a strange thing happened – the trapped employees decided to make the best of the situation.

With a mix of desperation and humour, they turned the elevator into their own impromptu party, complete with singing, dancing, and even a makeshift game of charades. By the time the maintenance crew finally arrived to rescue them, they were all laughing so hard that they had tears in their eyes.

As I reflect on the many coffee mishaps and office accidents that have graced our workplace, I can't help but smile. While we strive for professionalism and productivity, it is these unintentional hilarities that bring us closer together, forging bonds that go beyond the confines of our daily tasks.

In the end, it's the shared laughter and the ability to find humour in the unexpected that make the office a place of camaraderie and joy. So, here's to the coffee mishaps, the printer pranks, and the elevator escapades – may they continue to remind us that even in the most mundane of places, life is full of surprises and laughter, just waiting to be discovered.

The Art of Impressing the Boss (Or Not)

In the world of office politics, there was one golden rule that everyone seemed to follow religiously – impress the boss at all costs. As a fresh-faced graduate stepping into the corporate arena, I was determined to master the art of boss-impressing with finesse and flair. Little did I know that my attempts at impressing the boss would lead to a series of comical misadventures that would leave me questioning my strategies and laughing at my own follies.

The first lesson I learned was that appearance mattered – the boss's first impression of you could make or break your career. Armed with this knowledge, I decided to invest in a new wardrobe that screamed "professionalism" and "success." I showed up to the office on my first day wearing a power suit that made me feel like a high-powered executive ready to take on the world.

However, the moment I stepped into the office, I realized that I had misjudged the dress code entirely. While my fellow colleagues were dressed in smart casual attire, I stood out like a sore thumb in my stiff suit and tie. It was like wearing a tuxedo to a beach party – utterly out of place.

As I walked past my boss's office, I caught a glimpse of him smirking at my outfit. Oh, the embarrassment!

But I refused to be discouraged. I was determined to impress him, even if it meant enduring a day of uncomfortable attire.

The next step in the art of boss-impressing was to showcase my skills and talents. I worked late into the night, crafting the perfect presentation to dazzle my boss during a team meeting. I was certain that my well-researched data and meticulously designed charts would leave him in awe of my abilities.

When the day of the presentation arrived, I stood confidently in front of the team, ready to deliver my masterpiece. But as I clicked the button to start the slideshow, disaster struck – the presentation froze, leaving me fumbling and panicking as I tried to fix the technical glitch.

My boss watched in bemusement as I struggled to regain control of the presentation. I could feel my face turning as red as a ripe tomato, and my confidence evaporated like water on a hot stove. In that moment, I became the epitome of unimpressiveness.

But I refused to let one mishap define my journey to impress the boss. I decided to take on additional responsibilities and volunteer for every project that came my way. I thought that by showing my dedication and work ethic, I would surely win the boss's favour.

One day, I was given the opportunity to organize a company event – a task that I saw as a chance to shine. I threw myself into the planning process with gusto, carefully coordinating every detail to perfection. From selecting the venue to arranging the catering, I was a whirlwind of efficiency.

But on the day of the event, chaos ensued. The catering company delivered the wrong menu, the decorations fell apart, and the keynote speaker cancelled at the last minute. It was like a comedy of errors, and I was the unfortunate ringmaster of this circus.

As I tried to salvage the event, my boss came to check on the progress. I tried to put on a brave face and assured him that everything was under control, but the mayhem around us told a different story. He simply patted me on the back and said, "Sometimes, things don't go as planned. It's how you handle the unexpected that matters."

Though his words were comforting, I couldn't help but feel like I had failed to impress him once again. But little did I know that my boss was observing more than just my ability to handle an event gone awry – he was paying attention to my resilience and determination.

As the weeks turned into months, I continued to stumble through my attempts to impress the boss. There were moments of success and moments of failure, but through it all, I learned to laugh at myself and embrace the imperfections that made me human.

One day, as I was rushing to meet a deadline, I accidentally spilled a cup of coffee all over my desk. In my frustration, I blurted out a string of expletives that echoed through the office. To my horror, I realized that my boss was standing right behind me.

I braced myself for a reprimand, but instead, he burst into laughter. "You know," he said with a grin, "sometimes, it's the little things that make the biggest impression."

And just like that, my boss's laughter became the soundtrack of my journey to impress him. I realized that he appreciated my dedication and hard work, but he also valued my ability to find humour in the everyday mishaps.

From that day forward, I stopped trying to impress the boss with grand gestures and instead focused on being true to myself. I continued to work hard and strive for excellence, but I also allowed myself to make mistakes and have a good laugh at the absurdities of office life.

As I embraced the art of boss-impressing with a newfound sense of authenticity, I realized that it wasn't about being perfect or trying to fit into a mold – it was about being genuine and showing up as my imperfect, quirky self.

So, here's to the art of impressing the boss (or not) – a journey filled with hilarity, mishaps, and the wisdom to find laughter in the most unexpected places. And in the end, I learned that the best way to impress the boss was to simply be myself, coffee spills, freezing presentations, and all.

Co-worker Chronicles

Quirky Characters I Met

In the vast landscape of office life, I encountered a diverse array of co-workers – a colourful cast of characters that brought humour, intrigue, and a touch of eccentricity to the daily grind. From the moment I stepped foot into the office, I knew I was about to embark on a journey of unforgettable encounters with some of the quirkiest individuals I had ever met.

First on the list of quirky co-workers was "Mr. Punctuality," an employee whose obsession with timeliness bordered on the absurd. He arrived at the office precisely at 8:00 AM every morning, without fail, and would stand by the clock, tapping his foot impatiently if anyone dared to be even a minute late.

His punctuality extended to meetings as well, where he would insist on starting promptly, even if half the attendees were still struggling to find a seat. I once made the mistake of being a few minutes late to one of his meetings, and I was greeted with a stern glare and a passive-aggressive comment about "respecting everyone's time."

But despite his rigid adherence to punctuality, Mr. Punctuality had a quirky charm that was hard to resist. He was like the office's very own timekeeping wizard, a guardian of order in a world of perpetual tardiness.

Next up was "The Office Whisperer," an enigmatic figure who seemed to communicate in hushed tones and mysterious gestures. Whenever a sensitive topic arose, people would seek out The Office Whisperer for advice, as if they possessed some secret wisdom that could solve any problem.

I once witnessed The Office Whisperer skilfully defuse a heated argument between two colleagues with nothing more than a gentle touch on the shoulder and a few whispered words. It was as if they had a magical ability to bring harmony to even the most contentious situations.

But what truly set The Office Whisperer apart was their uncanny ability to overhear gossip and office rumours from across the room. It was like they had superhuman hearing, and they would often share the juiciest titbits with a knowing smile, as if they were privy to some cosmic office secrets.

And then there was "The Snack Master," an office superhero whose superpower was an uncanny knack for stocking the pantry with an endless supply of delectable treats. From chocolate bars to gourmet popcorn, The Snack Master had a sixth sense for predicting the office's snack cravings.

One day, during a particularly stressful meeting, The Snack Master appeared with a tray of freshly baked cookies, as if by magic. The meeting suddenly became much more bearable, and it was hard not to believe that The Snack Master had orchestrated the whole thing.

But The Snack Master's generosity came with a price – they had an uncanny ability to guilt-trip everyone into contributing to the snack fund. No one could resist their puppy-dog eyes and persuasive pleas for "just a dollar or two" to keep the snacks flowing.

Of course, every office has its resident "Office Comedian," the jester who lightens the mood with their witty one-liners and hilarious antics. Ours was no exception, and we were lucky to have "The Jokester Extraordinaire" in our midst.

The Jokester had a joke for every occasion, and they never missed an opportunity to inject humour into the most mundane of office tasks. They could turn a boring email thread into a comedy sketch and liven up a dull meeting with their impeccable timing.

But The Jokester's sense of humour was not without its pitfalls. There were times when their jokes fell flat, leaving awkward silences and nervous laughter in their wake. But they took it all in stride, always ready with a self-deprecating quip to lighten the mood.

Among the quirkiest of co-workers was "The Office Fashionista," an employee whose wardrobe could rival that of a fashion magazine. Every day was a fashion show, with The Office Fashionista flaunting their latest designer outfits and perfectly coordinated accessories.

I often found myself secretly admiring The Office Fashionista's style while simultaneously wondering how they managed to find the time and money to curate such a fabulous wardrobe. It was like working alongside a fashion icon, and I couldn't help but feel a pang of fashion envy every time I saw them stroll into the office with effortless elegance.

But for all the quirks and eccentricities of my co-workers, I soon realized that it was these very traits that made the office a lively and entertaining place. Each quirky character brought their unique flavour to the workplace, adding spice to the daily routine and reminding us that work could be fun and exciting.

As I navigated the ups and downs of office life, I cherished the moments of camaraderie and laughter with my quirky co-workers. We shared inside jokes, bonded over office mishaps, and supported each other through the daily challenges.

In the end, it was the quirky characters I met along the way that made my office experience unforgettable. They taught me that work could be more than just a place to earn a pay check – it could also be a place of genuine connection, laughter, and shared experiences.

So, here's to the quirky co-workers who made my office life a memorable adventure – the punctual, the mysterious, the snack-loving, the comedic, and the fashion-forward. Each one brought a special kind of magic to the office, turning it into a place where quirks were celebrated, laughter was abundant, and the daily grind was anything but ordinary.

The Unofficial Office Olympics

In the heart of the office, hidden behind a veneer of professionalism, there existed a secret world known only to a select few – the world of the Unofficial Office Olympics. This covert event was a celebration of absurdity, a showcase of quirky talents, and a hilarious escape from the monotony of the daily grind.

The Unofficial Office Olympics were the brainchild of "The Office Rebel," a mischievous employee who believed that life at work could use a healthy dose of fun and games. Armed with a playful spirit and a mischievous twinkle in their eye, The Office Rebel began to orchestrate a series of unorthodox competitions that would put the official Olympic Games to shame.

The opening ceremony of the Unofficial Office Olympics was a sight to behold. The Office Rebel led the procession, waving a makeshift flag and wearing a hat adorned with random office supplies. The participants followed suit, marching through the office like a jubilant parade, each with their own absurd props and quirky gestures.

The first event was the "Desk Chair Dash," where contestants competed to push their wheeled office chairs through a makeshift obstacle course without crashing into walls or knocking over fellow participants. It was a chaotic race that left a trail of laughter and overturned stationery in its wake.

Next up was the "Stapler Toss," a competition that tested both accuracy and arm strength. Participants took turns flinging staplers across the office, aiming for a target taped to the wall. The resounding clunk of staplers hitting the target was oddly satisfying, even if most of them missed by a mile.

But the pièce de résistance of the Unofficial Office Olympics was the "Paper Airplane Grand Prix." The office was transformed into an aviation wonderland, with contestants crafting their paper masterpieces with precision and care. Each plane was a work of art, complete with intricate folds and artistic flourishes.

As the planes took flight, the office became a battlefield of floating paper missiles. Colleagues ducked and dodged, trying to avoid the incoming paper bombardment. The air was filled with a symphony of giggles and the sound of paper planes crashing into walls, desks, and occasionally, a surprised participant's head.

But amid the laughter and camaraderie, a fierce competitive spirit emerged. The Unofficial Office Olympics were not for the faint of heart. Participants strategized, honed their skills, and even engaged in some playful trash-talking. It was all in good fun, but make no mistake – everyone wanted to be crowned the Unofficial Office Olympics champion.

The "Pencil Balance Beam" was a test of finesse and stability. Contestants attempted to walk across a narrow beam made of lined notepads while balancing a pencil on their nose. The sight of colleagues tiptoeing along the beam, arms flailing for balance, was nothing short of comical.

The "Water Cooler Relay" was a hilarious twist on the classic relay race. Instead of passing a baton, participants had to pass a water cooler jug while wearing blindfolds. It was a guaranteed recipe for spills and giggles as colleagues stumbled around, trying to find their teammates and avoid collisions.

But perhaps the most uproarious event of all was the "Elevator Disco Dance-Off." Contestants were challenged to turn the office elevator into a dance floor, complete with funky moves and exuberant dance-offs. The elevator became a disco ball-lit stage, and the participants unleashed their inner dance divas, showing off moves they never knew they had.

The Elevator Disco Dance-Off attracted quite an audience, with colleagues crowding around the elevator doors to witness the dance spectacle. The rhythmic thumping of the elevator doors added an unexpected beat to the music, creating a hilarious symphony of sound and movement.

As the Unofficial Office Olympics came to a close, The Office Rebel announced the winners with great fanfare, awarding each champion a medal made from paper clips and sticky notes. The champions beamed with pride, wearing their medals like badges of honour.

But in truth, everyone who participated in the Unofficial Office Olympics was a winner. The games had brought the office together in a way that no team-building exercise or motivational seminar ever could. Colleagues who had once been strangers bonded over laughter and shared silliness, forming friendships that would extend beyond the office walls.

In the days that followed, the Unofficial Office Olympics became the stuff of legend – a tale of absurdity and camaraderie passed down from one group of employees to the next. The office culture underwent a subtle shift, becoming a more light-hearted and joyful place.

And so, in the heart of the office, the Unofficial Office Olympics lived on, an annual tradition of laughter, camaraderie, and the celebration of quirky talents. The games were a reminder that even in the most serious and mundane of environments, there was room for playfulness, creativity, and the magic of the absurd.

As The Office Rebel once said, "Life is too short to take everything seriously. Sometimes, you just have to embrace the silliness and let laughter be your guide." And so, in the spirit of the Unofficial Office Olympics, we laughed, we played, and we celebrated the quirky characters we met along the way. For it was in these moments of joy and connection that we discovered the true essence of the office community – a place where friendships bloomed, spirits soared, and the Unofficial Office Olympics would forever reign as the champion of absurdity and merriment.

Email Etiquette Fails

Lessons in Tactful Messaging

In the digital age of the office, email had become the primary mode of communication – a tool that connected colleagues near and far with just a click of a button. But with great power came great responsibility, and many of us had to learn the hard way that mastering email etiquette was no easy feat.

It all began with "The Emoji Enthusiast," a colleague whose emails were a veritable emoji explosion. Every message was adorned with a barrage of smiley faces, thumbs-up, and heart emojis. It was like receiving a virtual rainbow with every email, and decoding the meaning behind the emojis became a fun yet perplexing challenge.

But The Emoji Enthusiast's enthusiasm didn't stop at emojis alone. They were also fond of using excessive exclamation marks, turning even the most mundane emails into virtual fireworks displays. Each sentence ended with a triumphant exclamation mark, as if every email was a cause for celebration!

As amusing as it was, The Emoji Enthusiast's email style had its pitfalls. It was hard to take their emails seriously, and important messages often got lost amidst the sea of emojis and exclamation marks. The rest of us had to resist the urge to respond with our own emoji-studded emails just to keep up with the trend.

Then there was "The Caps Lock Crusader," an employee whose emails were always written in capital letters. It was as if they were perpetually shouting at us through the computer screen. The Caps Lock Crusader's emails were impossible to ignore, but they also left us feeling like we were under constant attack.

One day, they accidentally sent an email to the entire office with the caps lock on. The result was an email that read like a digital scream, with colleagues scrambling to turn down the volume on their computers. Needless to say, The Caps Lock Crusader became a cautionary tale for the rest of us about the dangers of excessive caps lock usage.

But perhaps the most notorious of all email etiquette fails was "The Accidental Reply All Champion." We all knew them – the colleague who seemed to have a knack for hitting the dreaded "reply all" button at the worst possible moments.

The Accidental Reply All Champion's emails were a source of both amusement and exasperation. They would respond to innocuous office announcements with personal comments meant for just one person, leaving the entire office privy to their private conversations.

One day, in a particularly cringe-worthy incident, The Accidental Reply All Champion accidentally sent an email meant for their significant other to the entire office. The email was full of sweet nothings and romantic promises, and the office erupted into a flurry of laughter and teasing.

But The Accidental Reply All Champion took the embarrassment in stride, admitting their mistake and sending a follow-up email apologizing for the accidental overshare. From that day forward, they became the office's official reminder to double-check recipients before hitting "send."

Of course, email etiquette fails were not limited to the realm of emojis and caps lock. "The Grammar Guru" was another fascinating character, whose emails were meticulously edited for spelling and grammar errors. They took great pride in their linguistic prowess and had no qualms about pointing out the mistakes of others.

One day, I received an email from The Grammar Guru, complete with a list of corrections and suggestions for improvement. While their intentions were noble, it was hard not to feel like I was back in English class, getting a grammar lesson from a stern teacher.

The Grammar Guru's penchant for perfection was both impressive and intimidating. We all found ourselves carefully proofreading our emails before sending them to avoid becoming the next target of their red pen.

But amidst the email etiquette fails and moments of hilarity, we also discovered some valuable lessons in tactful messaging. "The Diplomatic Communicator" was a prime example of how to navigate the delicate world of office email with finesse.

The Diplomatic Communicator had a way of crafting emails that were clear, concise, and respectful. They knew how to address sensitive issues with grace and tact, using polite language and thoughtful phrasing to avoid misunderstandings.

One day, when a disagreement arose over a project, The Diplomatic Communicator stepped in and diffused the situation with their diplomatic email skills. They listened to both sides, acknowledged different perspectives, and proposed a compromise that satisfied everyone involved.

As we observed The Diplomatic Communicator's email finesse, we began to realize that effective communication was not just about the words we used, but also about the tone and approach we took. The art of tactful messaging was a delicate balance of clarity, respect, and empathy.

Armed with this newfound wisdom, we started to apply these lessons in our own emails. We resisted the urge to flood our messages with emojis and exclamation marks, and instead, focused on conveying our thoughts with clarity and professionalism.

We double-checked our recipients before sending emails and made a conscious effort to avoid the dreaded "reply all" button unless absolutely necessary. The office became a more harmonious place, with email exchanges that were both effective and tactful.

And so, in the realm of email etiquette fails, we found not just moments of humour, but also valuable lessons in communication. The quirks and missteps of our co-workers reminded us that even in the digital age, human interactions mattered.

As we navigated the world of office email, we learned to embrace our own quirks while also being mindful of how our messages were received. The Unofficial Office Olympics of email etiquette had taught us that behind every email was a person with feelings, and a little tact and thoughtfulness could go a long way in fostering positive connections.

And so, we bid farewell to the era of excessive emojis, caps lock crusades, and accidental reply all mishaps, and welcomed a new era of tactful messaging – one where clarity, respect, and empathy ruled the digital realm of office communication.

The Mystery of the Missing Office Supplies

In the heart of the office, a curious case had captured the attention of the entire workplace – the mystery of the missing office supplies. Pens, notepads, staplers, and even the occasional mouse pad had disappeared without a trace, leaving the office in a state of bewilderment and confusion.

The first sign of trouble came when "The Pen Detective" discovered that their favourite pen had vanished from their desk. At first, they brushed it off as a simple oversight, assuming they had misplaced it during a moment of absentmindedness. But as more pens began to disappear, The Pen Detective's suspicions grew, and they set out on a mission to uncover the truth.

With a magnifying glass and a notepad in hand, The Pen Detective conducted interviews with colleagues and searched for clues around the office. They even considered dusting for fingerprints on their desk, only to realize that the office was far too clean for that level of detective work.

But The Pen Detective was not alone in their pursuit of the truth. Other employees had noticed the strange phenomenon and joined forces to form the "Office Supply Sleuths." Together, they brainstormed theories and created elaborate charts mapping out the missing supplies.

"The Case of the Vanishing Notepads" seemed to be the most intriguing mystery of all. An entire shipment of notepads had mysteriously disappeared from the storage room, leaving the Office Supply Sleuths scratching their heads. The room had been locked, and there were no signs of forced entry, leading them to consider the possibility of an inside job.

One theory suggested that "The Paper Clip Ninja" might be behind the office supply heist. Known for their stealthy ways, The Paper Clip Ninja had a reputation for sneaking up on colleagues and attaching paper clips to their clothing when they least expected it. Their skills as a ninja were unparalleled, and some believed they had expanded their craft to stealing office supplies.

As the Office Supply Sleuths delved deeper into the case, they stumbled upon an unexpected lead. "The Sticky Note Enthusiast" had been acting particularly suspicious lately, hoarding stacks of sticky notes in their desk drawer. When questioned, they claimed it was just a harmless collection, but the sleuths were not convinced.

To gather more evidence, The Pen Detective and the Office Supply Sleuths decided to set a trap. They carefully placed a hidden camera near the office supplies to catch the culprit in the act. It was like something out of a spy movie, and they couldn't help but feel a rush of excitement as they waited for the mystery to unravel.

But as the days went by, the hidden camera revealed nothing but ordinary office activity. The office supplies remained untouched, and there was no sign of any culprit in action. It was as if the missing supplies had vanished into thin air, leaving the Office Supply Sleuths even more perplexed.

Just when they were about to give up hope, a breakthrough occurred. One day, while taking a stroll through the office, The Pen Detective noticed something unusual – "The Desk Drawer Hoarder" was surrounded by stacks of office supplies. Their desk was like a treasure trove of pens, notepads, and even a missing mouse pad.

The Pen Detective discreetly observed The Desk Drawer Hoarder's actions, and their suspicions were confirmed. The Desk Drawer Hoarder was indeed behind the missing office supplies. They had been secretly stockpiling supplies for reasons unknown, turning their desk into a hidden supply depot.

With the evidence in hand, The Pen Detective and the Office Supply Sleuths confronted The Desk Drawer Hoarder, who confessed to their hoarding habits. It turned out that they had a fear of running out of supplies and wanted to be prepared for any office supply shortage.

The revelation left the office in stitches of laughter. The mystery of the missing office supplies had been solved, and it was all thanks to The Pen Detective and the Office Supply Sleuths. The Desk Drawer Hoarder agreed to return the supplies to their rightful places, and the office supplies were finally at peace.

But the case of the missing office supplies had a surprising twist. As the news spread throughout the office, other employees confessed to their own quirky supply habits. "The Sticky Fingers Typist" admitted to having a habit of accidentally taking pens home and returning them weeks later, while "The Notepad Artist" confessed to using notepads for doodling rather than taking notes.

It turned out that the office supply mystery had been a manifestation of everyone's unique quirks and habits. The missing supplies were not a result of theft or conspiracy but rather a series of harmless mishaps and peculiarities.

In the end, the office came to embrace the quirkiness of its employees and even started a supply sharing program to prevent future supply shortages. The Pen Detective and the Office Supply Sleuths had unwittingly brought the office closer together, turning a mystery into a celebration of individuality and camaraderie.

As the office returned to its usual rhythm, The Pen Detective continued to keep a watchful eye on the office supplies, but now with a sense of humour and understanding. They had learned that sometimes the best solutions were found not through magnifying glasses and hidden cameras but through laughter and the appreciation of the quirks that made each employee unique.

And so, the mystery of the missing office supplies remained a light-hearted tale in the annals of the office's history – a reminder that even in the most mundane of places, there was room for laughter, camaraderie, and a touch of mystery. As the Office Supply Sleuths put away their detective tools, they knew that they had not just solved a mystery but also unravelled the delightful enigma of human quirks and the magic they brought to the workplace.

Break Room Banter

Surviving Lunchtime Conversations

In the heart of the office, the break room was both a haven of respite and a battleground of social interactions. Lunchtime conversations were a delightful yet perilous affair, where navigating through a maze of quirky colleagues and peculiar topics required finesse and a sense of humour.

The break room was a microcosm of the office's diverse personalities, each with their unique quirks and conversation styles. At the centre of it all was "The Lunchtime Orator," a colleague with a penchant for turning every lunch break into a one-person TED talk. Whether it was the latest office gossip or their own musings on the universe, The Lunchtime Orator had a gift for captivating their audience with eloquence and theatrical gestures.

One day, as I sat in the break room, trying to enjoy a peaceful lunch, The Lunchtime Orator spotted me and pounced on the opportunity to share their latest theories on time travel. With wild gesticulations and an abundance of scientific jargon, they painted a vivid picture of parallel universes and wormholes.

I tried to follow along, nodding politely, but my mind soon drifted to more pressing matters, like whether I had packed enough snacks to survive the day. However, escaping The Lunchtime Orator's captivating monologue proved to be a challenge.

As I glanced around the break room for a possible escape route, I locked eyes with "The Food Critic," a colleague whose lunchtime hobby was critiquing everyone's meals. They had a habit of peeking into colleagues' lunchboxes and offering unsolicited reviews on the nutritional value and presentation of their food.

"The Lunchtime Orator is on a roll," The Food Critic whispered, taking a bite of their meticulously crafted salad. "Their theories on time travel are almost as fascinating as this dressing."

I chuckled, grateful for The Food Critic's diversion. With their quick wit and playful sarcasm, they provided a refreshing break from the intensity of The Lunchtime Orator's lectures.

As the lunchtime banter continued, "The Comedian" joined the fray. With a knack for one-liners and impeccable timing, The Comedian brought laughter to the break room like a stand-up comedy show. They had an uncanny ability to find humour in the most mundane of office experiences, turning everyday mishaps into comedic gold.

When The Comedian noticed The Lunchtime Orator passionately discussing the intricacies of time travel, they couldn't resist interjecting with a quip, "If only we could travel back in time to get more coffee for this meeting."

The break room erupted into laughter, and even The Lunchtime Orator couldn't help but crack a smile. It was a moment of light-heartedness that brought some relief to the intensity of the lunchtime conversations.

But just as I thought I could finally enjoy my lunch in peace, "The Lunchtime Puzzler" approached, armed with a stack of brain teasers and riddles. They loved nothing more than challenging colleagues with their mind-bending puzzles, turning lunchtime into a cerebral workout.

"Alright, everyone, gather around," The Lunchtime Puzzler announced with a mischievous grin. "I've got a real brain teaser for you today."

Before I could protest, The Lunchtime Puzzler launched into a riddle involving a fox, a chicken, and a bag of grain that needed to be transported across a river in a boat. My brain struggled to keep up with the twists and turns of the puzzle, and I found myself contemplating the complexities of river-crossing strategies instead of savouring my lunch.

Just when I thought my brain might explode from the mental gymnastics, "The Office DJ" swooped in to save the day. Armed with a portable speaker, they began playing a lively playlist that instantly transformed the break room into a dance floor.

"Enough with the brain teasers! Let's have some fun," The Office DJ exclaimed, inviting everyone to let loose and dance away their lunchtime stress.

I happily joined in the impromptu dance party, shaking off the mental cobwebs and embracing the joy of the moment. The break room banter had taken an unexpected turn, and I realized that surviving lunchtime conversations didn't always mean escaping them but rather embracing the spontaneity and camaraderie they brought.

As the dance party wound down, "The Office Chef" entered the break room, bearing a platter of freshly baked cookies. Their culinary creations were legendary in the office, and everyone eagerly lined up to sample the sweet treats.

With mouths full of cookies, the break room banter resumed, but this time, it was more relaxed and filled with shared laughter. The Lunchtime Orator shared a humorous story about their attempts at baking cookies and how it turned into a kitchen disaster.

"The Office Chef's cookies are like works of art compared to mine," The Lunchtime Orator quipped, eliciting laughter from all of us.

As lunchtime drew to a close, I reflected on the colourful cast of characters I had encountered in the break room. From The Lunchtime Orator's passionate speeches to The Food Critic's culinary critiques, The Comedian's witty humour, The Lunchtime Puzzler's brain teasers, and The Office DJ's impromptu dance parties, each colleague brought their unique flair to the lunchtime conversations.

Surviving lunchtime banter wasn't about avoiding it but rather embracing the quirks and idiosyncrasies that made the office a lively and entertaining place. The break room was not just a space for lunch but a stage for camaraderie, laughter, and shared experiences that brought us closer together as a quirky, yet tight-knit, office community.

As I packed up my lunchbox and headed back to my desk, I knew that the break room banter would continue to be a delightful adventure of unexpected encounters and laughter-filled moments. So, here's to surviving lunchtime conversations – a comedic journey that made the office not just a place of work but a place of genuine connections and memorable lunchtime escapades.

The Rise and Fall of My Tangled Phone Calls

In the annals of office history, my phone calls were notorious – infamous, even. It all started innocently enough, with the occasional misdial or accidental butt dial. But little did I know that my tangled phone calls would soon become a comedy of errors that would leave the office in stitches of laughter.

It all began on a seemingly ordinary Monday morning. Armed with my cup of coffee and a to-do list, I settled into my desk and picked up the phone to make a routine call. But as I dialled the number, my finger slipped, and instead of reaching my intended contact, I found myself connected to "The Office Prankster."

Before I could react, The Office Prankster answered the phone with a fake British accent, pretending to be a posh receptionist. "Good morning, you've reached the office of Sir Chucklehead. How may I assist you today?"

Confused and slightly amused, I played along, "Um, yes, I believe I must have dialled the wrong number. I was trying to reach the accounting department."

"Oh, terribly sorry, madam. Let me transfer you right away," The Office Prankster replied, still maintaining the comedic British accent.

As the call was transferred, I couldn't help but chuckle at the unexpected encounter. Little did I know that this was just the beginning of my tangled phone call adventures.

The next day, I was determined to dial the correct number and avoid any further mishaps. But as fate would have it, the universe had other plans. This time, instead of misdialling, I accidentally hit the speakerphone button just as "The Conference Room Conductor" was leading a meeting.

Suddenly, my voice echoed through the conference room, interrupting The Conference Room Conductor's presentation. "Uh, sorry, sorry! That was a mistake!" I stammered, frantically hitting the end call button.

The conference room erupted into laughter, and The Conference Room Conductor graciously waved off the interruption, "No worries, just a little surprise serenade to brighten up the meeting."

Embarrassed but also amused, I sheepishly returned to my work, hoping that my phone call mishaps would end there. But it seemed that my phone had a mischievous mind of its own.

One day, I received a voicemail notification, and eagerly pressed the play button. To my horror, I realized that instead of recording my own voicemail message, my phone had captured a snippet of a private conversation I was having with a colleague about weekend plans.

The voicemail played back the sound of my voice discussing brunch plans and joking about my questionable cooking skills. Mortified, I immediately deleted the voicemail and considered changing my phone's voicemail password to avoid any future accidental broadcasts of my personal life.

But my tangled phone calls were not just limited to mishaps within the office. During a particularly hectic day, I was multitasking like a pro – typing an email, drinking coffee, and talking on the phone all at once. However, my multitasking prowess failed me when I accidentally spilled coffee on my desk and knocked my phone onto the floor.

In a desperate attempt to catch the falling phone, I accidentally hit the speakerphone button, connecting me to "The Office Gossip" just as they were in the midst of sharing a juicy titbit with a fellow colleague.

My heart sank as I heard The Office Gossip's voice loud and clear through the speakerphone, revealing a piece of confidential information meant for their colleague's ears only. I quickly picked up the phone and ended the call, hoping that no damage had been done.

To my relief, The Office Gossip didn't seem to notice the accidental eavesdropping, and I made a mental note to be more cautious with my coffee and phone juggling skills in the future.

As the days turned into weeks, my tangled phone calls became legendary among my colleagues. They would gather around the break room, swapping stories of my phone call mishaps and sharing their own tales of phone-related comedy.

"The Phone Prank Master" even approached me with a proposal to collaborate on a series of comedic phone call pranks. While I appreciated the humour, I politely declined, realizing that my phone call adventures were entertaining enough without any intentional pranks.

But just as my tangled phone calls had risen to fame, they eventually met their downfall. After a particularly hectic week, I had finally managed to go a full day without any phone call mishaps, feeling like I had triumphed over the phone's mischievous tendencies.

But the universe had one last twist in store for me. As I was leaving the office, I reached into my bag to grab my phone, only to realize that it was nowhere to be found. Panic set in as I retraced my steps, frantically asking colleagues if they had seen my phone.

It turned out that I had left it on my desk, and The Office Prankster had decided to play one last prank. They had taken my phone and hidden it in the break room fridge, leaving a note that read, "For your tangled phone call adventures – a chilling surprise!"

With a mixture of relief and exasperation, I retrieved my phone from the break room fridge, knowing that my tangled phone call saga had come to an end. While the misadventures were at times embarrassing and inconvenient, they had also brought laughter and camaraderie to the office.

As I reflected on the rise and fall of my tangled phone calls, I realized that sometimes life's little mishaps were the source of unexpected moments of connection and joy. And so, with a smile and a touch of fond nostalgia, I bid farewell to my phone call misadventures, knowing that they would forever be a quirky part of my office journey.

The Bizarre World of Company Jargon

In the realm of the office, a peculiar language existed – a strange and mysterious dialect known as company jargon. It was a world of buzzwords, acronyms, and nonsensical phrases that could leave even the most seasoned employees scratching their heads in bewilderment. As I navigated through the bizarre world of company jargon, I quickly learned that understanding this enigmatic language was both a challenge and a source of endless amusement.

It all began on my first day at the office, when I was introduced to "The Jargon Enthusiast," a colleague who seemed to have a master's degree in company-speak. They greeted me with a warm smile and a barrage of jargon-laden phrases, leaving me feeling like I had stumbled into a foreign land with no guidebook.

"Welcome to the team! We're all about synergy, disruptive innovation, and leveraging our core competencies," The Jargon Enthusiast proclaimed, their enthusiasm matched only by my utter confusion.

I nodded along, trying my best to appear knowledgeable about this strange language, but inside, I was frantically Googling the meanings of "synergy" and "core competencies." Little did I know that this was just the beginning of my journey into the bizarre world of company jargon.

As the days turned into weeks, I encountered an array of baffling jargon phrases that seemed to permeate every office conversation. "Let's touch base on our deliverables and circle back to discuss the action items," "We need to think outside the box and pivot our strategy," and "This project is a game-changer that will disrupt the market" became commonplace phrases that left me feeling like I had fallen into a never-ending loop of nonsense.

But perhaps the most perplexing of all was "The Buzzword Bingo Champion," a colleague who had created a bingo card filled with company jargon phrases. During meetings, The Buzzword Bingo Champion would discreetly check off the phrases as they were uttered, and when they had a full row, they would quietly mutter, "Bingo."

One day, I decided to join in the game and created my own buzzword bingo card. Little did I know that the office would soon be gripped by a silent competition of trying to fill our bingo cards during meetings without being caught.

The result was a room full of employees trying to casually drop jargon phrases into conversations, leading to hilariously forced discussions about "synergizing our growth opportunities" and "optimizing our bandwidth for maximum productivity."

As the buzzword bingo game continued, we found ourselves creating new jargon phrases just to check off our bingo cards. The office became a cacophony of nonsensical jargon, and meetings turned into a comical display of linguistic acrobatics.

But beyond the laughter and amusement, I couldn't help but wonder if company jargon served any real purpose or if it was merely a façade to make the mundane sound profound. "The Jargon Philosopher" was a colleague who pondered this very question, often engaging in deep discussions about the true meaning of jargon and its impact on office culture.

"The language we use shapes our thoughts and perceptions," The Jargon Philosopher mused. "Company jargon may be a form of linguistic tribalism, a way for us to feel like we belong to a special group with its own secret language."

Their words struck a chord, and I realized that company jargon was more than just a collection of meaningless phrases – it was a reflection of office culture and a way for employees to bond over shared experiences and challenges.

As my understanding of company jargon deepened, I also became privy to its darker side – the "Jargon Overload." It happened during a particularly intense meeting when The Jargon Enthusiast and The Buzzword Bingo Champion engaged in a battle of linguistic prowess, trying to outdo each other with the most convoluted jargon phrases.

The result was a rapid-fire exchange of buzzwords and acronyms that left the rest of us struggling to keep up. It was like a jargon hurricane had swept through the room, leaving us dazed and confused.

"I can't take it anymore! My brain is on jargon overload!" "The Office Rebel" finally exclaimed, breaking the tension with a burst of laughter.

The Office Rebel had a knack for cutting through the jargon and bringing us back to reality. Their irreverent humour and ability to speak plainly amidst the sea of jargon were a breath of fresh air in the office.

Inspired by The Office Rebel's defiance of the jargon overload, I decided to take a stand against the jargon myself. During meetings, I made a conscious effort to speak plainly and avoid using jargon phrases just for the sake of sounding impressive.

To my surprise, others followed suit, and we found ourselves engaging in more authentic and meaningful conversations. The bizarre world of company jargon had not only entertained us but also taught us a valuable lesson in communication – that sometimes, simplicity and clarity were far more effective than a barrage of buzzwords.

And so, as I continued my journey through the strange world of company jargon, I did so with a newfound sense of humour and a willingness to challenge the jargon status quo. The office culture remained quirky, but we had learned to embrace our own unique language and find meaning in genuine connections – without the need for a jargon dictionary. For, in the end, the true language of the office was not found in buzzwords and acronyms but in the laughter, camaraderie, and shared experiences that made our workplace a truly bizarre and delightful world of its own.

Office Pranks Gone Wild

In the realm of the office, where staplers and sticky notes roamed freely, a mischievous spirit dwelled among the cubicles – The Office Prankster. Armed with a wicked sense of humour and a penchant for practical jokes, The Office Prankster was both feared and revered for their legendary pranks. From harmless hijinks to elaborate escapades, their antics had become the stuff of office folklore. But little did we know that one day, their pranks would go wild, taking the office by storm.

It all began innocently enough, with a classic prank involving "The Phantom Printer." The Office Prankster had devised a cunning plan to sneak into colleagues' offices and replace their printer paper with an endless roll of joke paper – a never-ending stream of cat memes, cheesy pick-up lines, and funny quotes.

The unsuspecting victims couldn't help but laugh at the quirky surprise that awaited them when they tried to print their important documents. What started as a simple prank soon became a battle of wits, as The Phantom Printer and The Office Prankster engaged in a hilarious game of prank-tag, each trying to outwit the other with even more inventive printer antics.

As the pranks escalated, The Office Prankster set their sights on "The Office Grouch" – a colleague known for their perpetually grumpy demeanour. Armed with a battalion of office supplies and a dose of creativity, The Office Prankster transformed The Office Grouch's desk into a whimsical wonderland overnight.

When The Office Grouch arrived the next morning, they were greeted with a desk adorned with balloons, streamers, and a neon sign that read, "Grouchville: Population 1." The transformation was so absurdly over-the-top that even The Office Grouch couldn't help but crack a smile.

But as laughter echoed through the office, we soon learned that The Office Prankster had unleashed a storm of mischief that would sweep us all into their wild pranks. It started with "The Coffee Caper," where The Office Prankster teamed up with "The Office Chef" to concoct a devious plot.

One fateful morning, The Office Chef brewed a pot of "mystery coffee," complete with exotic spices and questionable ingredients. The Office Prankster managed to distract The Coffee Connoisseur – a colleague known for their discerning taste in coffee – while The Office Chef replaced their usual brew with the mysterious concoction.

The Coffee Connoisseur took a cautious sip of the mystery coffee, and their face contorted in surprise. "What is this? Is this a prank?" they demanded, glancing around the office suspiciously.

The Office Prankster and The Office Chef exchanged knowing glances, and before anyone could confess, they burst into laughter, revealing their collaboration in The Coffee Caper.

"What can I say? Sometimes, you have to spice things up in the office," The Office Chef quipped, handing The Coffee Connoisseur a freshly brewed cup of their favourite coffee.

From that day on, it seemed like every corner of the office had become fair game for pranks. "The Sticky Situation" saw The Office Prankster ingeniously covering a colleague's chair with sticky notes, turning it into a vibrant mosaic of colours. "The Mouse Prank" involved swapping mouse buttons and leaving colleagues puzzled over the reversed functionality.

Even "The Office Plants" weren't spared from The Office Prankster's antics. One day, The Office Prankster created a forest of inflatable palm trees and placed them strategically around the office, turning the once-quiet space into a tropical oasis.

"The Office Wildlife Sanctuary" was another bizarre prank that involved placing stuffed animals throughout the office – from cuddly kittens to menacing alligators. Colleagues found themselves stumbling upon the "wildlife" in the most unexpected places, sparking laughter and confusion.

But perhaps the wildest prank of all was "The Cubicle Transformation," where The Office Prankster enlisted the help of everyone in the office to redecorate a colleague's cubicle while they were away on vacation.

The unsuspecting colleague returned to find their cubicle had been transformed into a beach paradise, complete with a mini sandbox, beach chairs, and a fake palm tree. As the colleague sat in their beach-themed cubicle, they couldn't help but feel like they had stepped into a surreal vacation getaway.

But just as we thought The Office Prankster had reached the peak of their wild pranks, they unveiled their pièce de résistance – "The Great Office Water Balloon Battle." It started innocently enough with a small water balloon ambush, but it quickly escalated into an all-out water balloon war.

Colleagues armed themselves with water balloons, water guns, and even makeshift water cannons crafted from office supplies. The office became a battlefield of laughter and camaraderie, as we all let loose in the wildest office water balloon fight in history.

As water balloons splashed, laughter echoed, and friendships deepened, I realized that The Office Prankster's wild pranks had brought us closer together as a team. In the midst of the chaos and hilarity, we found a sense of unity and joy that transcended the boundaries of cubicles and job titles.

As The Office Prankster took a bow, their pranks had left an indelible mark on the office culture. We had become a quirky community bound not only by work but also by laughter, shared memories, and the occasional water balloon skirmish.

And so, as I reflect on the chapter of "Office Pranks Gone Wild," I do so with a heart full of gratitude for The Office Prankster's mischievous spirit. Their pranks may have been wild and unconventional, but they had woven a tapestry of laughter and camaraderie that had transformed our office into a place of joy and genuine connections.

As we brace ourselves for the next wave of pranks, we do so with a smile, knowing that The Office Prankster's antics have taught us the true value of embracing humour and light-heartedness in the often serious world of work. For in the end, it's not just the tasks we accomplish but the laughter we share that makes our office journey truly unforgettable.

The Caffeine Conundrum

Tales of a Coffee Addict

In the bustling realm of the office, there was a curious creature – The Coffee Addict. Armed with a trusty coffee mug and a never-ending quest for the perfect brew, The Coffee Addict navigated the daily grind with a healthy dose of caffeine and a dash of humour. But little did they know that their caffeine-fuelled adventures would soon lead them into a conundrum of comedic proportions.

It all began on a particularly hectic Monday morning. The Coffee Addict stumbled into the office, bleary-eyed and in desperate need of their morning fix. But to their horror, the office coffee machine had decided to go on strike, emitting nothing more than a pitiful sputter of lukewarm liquid.

"It's a coffee catastrophe!" The Coffee Addict exclaimed, staring at the malfunctioning machine in disbelief.

But as they say, necessity is the mother of invention. Determined to fuel their caffeine addiction, The Coffee Addict resorted to drastic measures. Armed with a French press, a bag of coffee beans, and a hopeful heart, they embarked on a quest to brew their own coffee.

As the office looked on in amusement, The Coffee Addict clumsily navigated through the brewing process. Coffee grounds ended up scattered across the counter, and water splashed everywhere as they attempted to master the art of the French press.

"The Coffee Scientist" – a colleague renowned for their coffee expertise – couldn't help but intervene. "Allow me to assist you in your noble coffee endeavour," they offered with a chuckle.

With The Coffee Scientist's guidance, The Coffee Addict managed to brew a passable cup of coffee. It may not have been perfect, but it was a caffeinated triumph in the face of adversity.

From that day on, The Coffee Addict became a master of coffee improvisation. They experimented with various brewing methods – from pour-over to cold brew – and even attempted to create their own signature coffee blend, which they affectionately called "The Caffeine Concoction."

But as The Coffee Addict delved deeper into their coffee obsession, they encountered a conundrum that every caffeine lover faced – "The Coffee Tolerance Tangle." It started innocently enough, with a daily cup of coffee to kickstart the morning.

But soon, one cup turned into two, then three, and before they knew it, The Coffee Addict found themselves trapped in an endless cycle of caffeine consumption.

"I can quit coffee anytime I want," The Coffee Addict declared with a hint of defiance, holding their fourth cup of the day.

But their claim was put to the test when "The Office Wellness Guru" issued a challenge — a week-long caffeine detox to break free from The Coffee Tolerance Tangle.

The Office Wellness Guru presented The Coffee Addict with herbal teas, green smoothies, and a variety of caffeine-free alternatives. It was a test of willpower and a battle against the relentless call of caffeine.

As The Coffee Addict sipped their herbal tea with a wistful expression, they discovered a new appreciation for the ritual of coffee drinking — the aroma, the warmth, and the sense of comfort it brought.

"I miss the buzz of coffee, but this detox has made me realize that it's not just about the caffeine. It's about the experience and the joy of savouring a cup of coffee," The Coffee Addict admitted, their eyes glimmering with newfound wisdom.

But just as they thought they had conquered The Coffee Tolerance Tangle, temptation appeared in the form of "The Office Coffee Cart" — a mobile coffee vendor with an array of delicious caffeinated delights.

With a mixture of hesitation and excitement, The Coffee Addict approached the coffee cart, torn between staying true to their detox or surrendering to the allure of a freshly brewed cappuccino.

"I thought you were on a caffeine detox," The Office Wellness Guru teased, raising an eyebrow.

The Coffee Addict grinned sheepishly. "Just a little indulgence won't hurt, right?"

And so, they found themselves indulging in a single cup of coffee, savouring each sip as if it were a forbidden pleasure. The Office Wellness Guru, with a knowing smile, didn't chastise them but instead reminded them of the importance of balance and moderation.

As the week of the caffeine detox came to an end, The Coffee Addict emerged with a newfound appreciation for coffee and a sense of control over their caffeine intake. They had untangled themselves from The Coffee Tolerance Tangle and discovered the art of savouring coffee in moderation.

But their caffeine adventures didn't end there. The Coffee Addict soon encountered a new challenge – "The Office Coffee Machine Revolt." The trusty coffee machine, which had faithfully served the office for years, decided to go on strike once again.

"It's a coffee machine uprising!" The Coffee Addict declared, staring at the defiant machine.

With a determined spirit and a touch of caffeine-induced courage, they attempted to fix the machine, tinkering with its inner workings and banging on its sides in desperation.

But it seemed that The Office Coffee Machine had developed a personality of its own, and it refused to yield to The Coffee Addict's attempts at restoration.

"The Coffee Machine has spoken. It's time for a coffee break," The Office Prankster chimed in, causing a round of laughter among the office.

With the coffee machine out of commission, The Coffee Addict turned to alternative methods once again. They resorted to the French press, pour-over, and even an old-fashioned stovetop coffee maker.

As The Coffee Addict brewed coffee with a sense of determination and a hint of madness, they became a symbol of caffeine resilience and resourcefulness in the office.

And so, as The Coffee Addict's tales of caffeine-fuelled adventures continued, they taught us that coffee was more than just a beverage – it was a source of camaraderie, humour, and a daily dose of comfort in the midst of the office chaos.

As we laughed and sipped coffee together, we realized that The Coffee Addict's conundrum was not just about caffeine but about embracing life's quirks and finding joy in the little moments – whether it was the perfect cup of coffee or the unexpected detours in our daily routines.

And so, with a coffee mug in hand and a heart full of laughter, The Coffee Addict continued their caffeinated journey through the office, reminding us all to savour the simple pleasures and find humour in life's conundrums. For in the end, it's not just the caffeine that keeps us going, but the laughter, connections, and the delightful tales of The Caffeine

Conundrum that make our office journey truly unforgettable.

Awkward Encounters

Running into the Boss Outside the Office

In the vast expanse of the outside world, where office walls were replaced by bustling streets and busy cafes, there lurked an awkward encounter waiting to pounce on unsuspecting employees – the dreaded run-in with the boss outside the office. It was a scenario that sent shivers down the spines of even the most composed employees, for it meant navigating the treacherous waters of casual conversation with the person who held their professional fate in their hands.

One fateful Saturday afternoon, I decided to treat myself to a leisurely stroll in the park. Little did I know that fate had a different plan in store for me. As I basked in the tranquillity of nature, my heart skipped a beat when I spotted none other than "The Big Boss" approaching from a distance.

I immediately considered my options – Should I pretend not to see them and stealthily change direction? Should I pretend to be engrossed in my phone? Or should I suck it up and face the inevitable awkward encounter head-on?

In a moment of panic, I chose the last option, but as luck would have it, my attempt at nonchalance backfired spectacularly. I fumbled with my phone, accidentally dropping it, and promptly bumped into a tree.

"The Big Boss" stopped in their tracks, a puzzled expression on their face. "Are you alright?"

"Yes, just embracing my inner tree-hugger," I blurted out, cheeks flushing with embarrassment.

The Big Boss chuckled, and I could practically hear them filing away the awkward encounter in the mental archives of their memory.

As if that encounter wasn't enough, the universe seemed determined to test my composure further. The next week, I found myself running into The Big Boss once again, this time at the grocery store.

In a desperate bid to appear casual, I tried to focus on my shopping list, but my hand trembled as I reached for a carton of eggs, and it slipped from my grasp, rolling down the aisle and causing a minor egg-splosion.

"The Big Boss" arched an eyebrow, their lips twitching with amusement. "Looks like you're having an adventurous shopping trip."

"I like to keep things...eggciting," I replied, cringing inwardly at my terrible pun.

As I made a hasty retreat to the checkout counter, I couldn't help but wonder if I had somehow become a magnet for awkward encounters with The Big Boss.

But it seemed that I wasn't the only one afflicted by this phenomenon. "The Office Veteran" — a seasoned employee with a reputation for being unflappable – had their fair share of awkward encounters with The Big Boss.

One day, "The Office Veteran" recounted their own tale of running into The Big Boss at a concert. They had been trying to blend into the sea of concert-goers when they accidentally spilled their drink on The Big Boss's shoes.

"I thought I was in trouble for sure," "The Office Veteran" confessed. "But instead, The Big Boss just laughed it off and said they admired my enthusiasm."

It appeared that even The Big Boss wasn't immune to awkward encounters outside the office. "The Casual Encounter Specialist" – a colleague who had mastered the art of casual conversations – had their fair share of memorable run-ins.

Once, "The Casual Encounter Specialist" found themselves sharing an elevator with The Big Boss. In a moment of panic, they attempted to make small talk, only to end up complimenting The Big Boss on their choice of socks.

"The Casual Encounter Specialist" cringed at their blunder but was relieved when The Big Boss simply chuckled and said, "Well, I believe socks are a subtle expression of personality."

As we exchanged stories of awkward encounters, we realized that these mishaps were not a sign of incompetence or unprofessionalism, but rather a reminder of our shared humanity. The Big Boss was, after all, a person too – someone who could appreciate humour and understand that awkward encounters were a part of life.

Emboldened by this realization, I decided to face my next encounter with The Big Boss with a newfound sense of confidence. But as fate would have it, the encounter took place at a charity event, where we were both volunteers.

Determined to make a good impression, I volunteered to hand out snacks to attendees. But in a twist of fate, I accidentally knocked over the snack table, creating a snack avalanche that left us both covered in popcorn and potato chips.

I gaped at the mess before me, unsure of how to salvage the situation. But to my surprise, The Big Boss burst into laughter, their eyes crinkling with amusement.

"I guess this means we can add 'snack avalanche handler' to your list of talents," The Big Boss quipped, handing me a napkin to clean up the mess.

As we cleaned up the snack disaster together, I realized that awkward encounters could be opportunities for unexpected connections and shared laughter.

In the end, The Caffeine Conundrum, the office pranks gone wild, and the bizarre world of company jargon were all part of the rich tapestry of office life. They taught us that work wasn't just about tasks and deadlines but about laughter, camaraderie, and the joy of embracing life's quirks and conundrums.

And so, as I continued my journey through the office, I did so with a smile on my face and a heart full of laughter, knowing that no matter how awkward or chaotic things got, it was the moments of connection, humour, and shared experiences that made the office a truly special and unforgettable place.

The Great Printer Paper Jam Disaster

In the heart of the office, where the hum of computers and the clatter of keyboards echoed, there existed a technological beast – The Office Printer. This seemingly innocuous machine had a mischievous streak, lurking in the shadows, waiting for the perfect moment to strike. And so, it came to pass that one fateful day, The Great Printer Paper Jam Disaster unfolded, leaving the office in a state of chaotic hilarity.

The day started like any other, with the office buzzing with activity. As I approached The Office Printer to retrieve my freshly printed documents, I was met with a sight that sent a shiver down my spine – a blinking red light and an ominous error message on the display.

"Paper jam? How can this be?" I muttered, inspecting the printer for any visible signs of a jam.

Little did I know that The Office Printer was merely teasing me. As I opened the paper tray and checked the printer's inner workings, the paper jam seemed to magically disappear. I let out a sigh of relief, believing that I had thwarted the printer's mischievous plans.

But the joy was short-lived, for as I pressed the print button once more, The Great Printer Paper Jam Disaster struck again, and this time, it was determined to bring the office to its knees.

"The Office IT Guru" – a colleague who was well-versed in the ways of technology – came to my aid. Together, we embarked on a quest to free the trapped paper and liberate The Office Printer from its jammed state.

As we fiddled with levers and opened various compartments, The Office IT Guru explained the intricate inner workings of The Office Printer, complete with sound effects and dramatic gestures.

"We must navigate through the treacherous paper pathways and liberate the paper from its paper jam prison!" The Office IT Guru proclaimed.

It was a perilous journey, and with each attempt to dislodge the jammed paper, we were met with a stubborn resistance. The paper seemed to have a mind of its own, firmly wedged within the printer's labyrinthine passages.

As The Great Printer Paper Jam Disaster continued, a crowd of curious onlookers gathered around us, watching the spectacle with amusement. "The Office Cheerleader" – a colleague known for their unshakeable optimism – couldn't resist turning the situation into a cheer.

"Give me a P! Give me an A! Give me a P-E-R! What does that spell? PAPER JAM! Woo!" The Office Cheerleader chanted, leading the crowd in a cheer.

Amidst the laughter and camaraderie, The Office Printer showed no sign of surrender. It seemed that no matter how many paper jams we cleared, another one would inevitably follow.

"I think The Office Printer is toying with us," I muttered, wiping sweat from my brow.

"Just one more try!" The Office IT Guru urged, determination shining in their eyes.

And so, we pressed on, determined to conquer The Great Printer Paper Jam Disaster once and for all. But just as we were on the brink of victory, disaster struck again – this time, The Office Printer emitted a mournful whirring sound, and its display flashed an even more cryptic error message.

"Uh oh. I think we've made it mad," The Office IT Guru whispered, glancing nervously at the printer.

It was as if The Office Printer had declared war on us, and we were now locked in an epic battle of wits and technology. We tried every trick in the book, from gently coaxing the paper out to resorting to a slightly aggressive jiggle, but The Office Printer remained unyielding.

"The Office Prankster" couldn't resist adding to the hilarity, suggesting that we perform a printer exorcism, complete with chants and incantations to banish the paper jam demons.

"The Printer Spirit shall not be contained!" The Office Prankster proclaimed dramatically, waving a stapler as a makeshift wand.

Amidst the laughter and absurdity, I felt a glimmer of hope. Perhaps all we needed was a touch of whimsy to break the printer's spell.

With a newfound sense of determination and a sprinkle of whimsy, we devised an ingenious plan. "The Office Engineer" – a colleague who loved tinkering with gadgets – suggested a creative solution involving a modified paperclip and some office supplies.

As The Office Engineer skilfully wielded their makeshift tools, we held our breath, hoping that this time, the paper jam would meet its match.

And then, like a miracle, The Office Printer hummed to life, and a triumphant cheer erupted from the crowd.

"We did it! The Great Printer Paper Jam Disaster has been defeated!" The Office IT Guru declared, raising their arms in victory.

As we basked in the glory of our triumph, I realized that The Great Printer Paper Jam Disaster had been more than just a chaotic mishap. It had brought us together as a team, united in our quest to conquer the mischievous printer.

In the days that followed, we celebrated our victory with an impromptu "Office Printer Parade," complete with streamers and banners. The Office Printer was adorned with a "Conqueror of Paper Jams" sticker, a badge of honour for surviving The Great Printer Paper Jam Disaster.

And so, as I reflect on the chapter of The Great Printer Paper Jam Disaster, I do so with a smile on my face and a heart full of laughter. It was a tale of chaos, camaraderie, and the triumph of whimsy over technology.

For in the end, The Office Printer may have had a mischievous streak, but it also taught us the value of teamwork, humour, and the joy of overcoming challenges together – one paper jam at a time. And so, armed with a renewed sense of camaraderie, we ventured forth into the adventures that awaited us in the ever-quirky world of the office.

Meeting Madness

Anecdotes from Never-Ending Discussions

In the heart of the office, where time seemed to stretch endlessly and chairs groaned under the weight of restless employees, there lurked a formidable creature – The Never-Ending Meeting. Armed with an insatiable appetite for time and an unquenchable thirst for discussion, The Never-Ending Meeting was notorious for trapping employees in its clutches for hours on end. And so, it came to pass that Meeting Madness descended upon the office, leaving us with a treasure trove of amusing anecdotes from the depths of never-ending discussions.

The first tale of Meeting Madness began innocently enough, with a routine team meeting that was slated to last no more than an hour. "The Optimistic Timekeeper" – a colleague who always believed in the efficiency of meetings – confidently set the timer for an hour.

As the meeting progressed, it quickly became apparent that The Never-Ending Meeting had other plans. The agenda seemed to multiply with each passing minute, and every topic spiralled into a labyrinth of tangents and side discussions.

"The Optimistic Timekeeper" nervously adjusted the timer, extending the meeting duration to two hours. But even that proved to be wishful thinking, as The Never-Ending Meeting showed no signs of abating.

As the hours ticked by, the once-engaged participants began to display signs of Meeting Madness. "The Doodler" transformed their notepad into a work of art, doodling intricate patterns that bore no resemblance to the meeting's content.

"The Nodding Napper" – a colleague known for their occasional catnaps during meetings – succumbed to the allure of drowsiness, attempting to maintain a facade of attentiveness with subtle head nods.

"The Office Daydreamer" gazed longingly out the window, imagining themselves on a tropical beach rather than being trapped in the never-ending discussion.

But perhaps the most amusing of all was "The Silent Observer" – a colleague who remained eerily quiet throughout the meeting, as if they had discovered the secret to avoiding Meeting Madness altogether.

As the meeting finally reached its conclusion, "The Optimistic Timekeeper" sheepishly turned off the timer, which now displayed a whopping four hours and counting. The room erupted in laughter, and we couldn't help but wonder if we had just experienced a time warp within the confines of the meeting room.

But the madness didn't end there. The Never-Ending Meeting continued to unleash its fury, and each subsequent gathering seemed to outdo the previous one in terms of absurdity.

"The Office Master of Distractions" – a colleague known for their uncanny ability to veer off-topic – managed to steer a discussion about project deadlines into an animated debate about the best pizza toppings.

"The Agenda Stickler" – a no-nonsense colleague who always adhered to the meeting agenda – found themselves outnumbered by a group of enthusiastic storytellers, turning a status update into a round of office anecdotes.

And then there was "The Meeting Foodie" – a colleague who believed in the power of snacks to combat Meeting Madness. Armed with an array of treats, The Meeting Foodie transformed every meeting into a gastronomic adventure.

As we munched on cookies and chips during the meetings, we couldn't help but feel that snacks were the unsung heroes in our battle against the tedium of never-ending discussions.

But perhaps the most memorable Meeting Madness anecdote involved "The Phantom Presenter" – a colleague who accidentally joined the wrong virtual meeting and ended up participating in a meeting with a completely different team.

"The Phantom Presenter" launched into their presentation with gusto, unaware of their mistake until someone gently reminded them that they were in the wrong meeting room.

As they hastily exited the virtual meeting, the rest of us burst into laughter, amazed by the serendipitous encounter. The Phantom Presenter later recounted their adventure, and we all agreed that it was a fitting tale of Meeting Madness at its finest.

But amidst the laughter and absurdity, we couldn't help but wonder if there was a remedy for Meeting Madness. "The Meeting Mediator" – a colleague known for their conflict resolution skills – suggested implementing strict time limits and setting clear agendas for meetings.

"The Meeting Mediator" also proposed the idea of "meeting mascots" – playful toys or objects that could be passed around during meetings to signify when someone was veering off-topic or speaking for too long.

"The Office Therapist" – a colleague who always knew how to lighten the mood – suggested implementing a "meeting dance break," where participants could take a quick dance break to re-energize during long discussions.

As we brainstormed creative solutions to combat Meeting Madness, we realized that humour and camaraderie were the ultimate weapons in our arsenal. Embracing the absurdity of never-ending discussions and finding ways to inject laughter into meetings made the experience more bearable.

And so, armed with our newfound sense of humour, we ventured forth into the world of never-ending meetings, ready to face Meeting Madness head-on.

We embraced the quirks and idiosyncrasies of our colleagues, turning each meeting into a shared adventure filled with laughter and camaraderie.

As we celebrated each small victory – whether it was successfully adhering to the meeting agenda or avoiding tangents – we realized that Meeting Madness was a challenge we could conquer together.

And so, the chapter of Meeting Madness came to a close, leaving us with a collection of amusing anecdotes and a newfound appreciation for the power of humour and unity in navigating the wild world of never-ending discussions.

For in the end, it wasn't just about surviving the meetings but about finding joy in the shared experience of facing Meeting Madness as a team. And armed with laughter and camaraderie, we were ready to take on whatever Meeting Madness the office had in store for us next.

The Office Party

A Comedy of Errors

In the heart of the office, where workstations transformed into dance floors and water coolers turned into makeshift punch stations, there existed an annual tradition that both excited and terrified employees – The Office Party. It was a time of celebration, camaraderie, and a comedy of errors that had become a hallmark of this much-anticipated event.

As the day of The Office Party approached, the office buzzed with excitement. "The Party Planner Extraordinaire" – a colleague known for their meticulous event planning skills – had spared no effort in creating an unforgettable evening for everyone.

The theme for this year's party was "Retro Night," and the office was decked out with disco balls, neon lights, and a playlist of nostalgic tunes. The atmosphere was electric as employees arrived, dressed in their best retro attire, ready to let loose and dance the night away.

But little did we know that The Office Party would be a comedy of errors from start to finish. It all began with "The DJ Dilemma" – an unforeseen hiccup that set the tone for the night's antics.

"The Party Planner Extraordinaire" had hired a DJ to spin the tunes and keep the dance floor alive. But as the party kicked off, we quickly realized that The DJ Dilemma had struck. The DJ seemed to have a unique taste in music, veering from '70s disco hits to obscure techno tracks that left us scratching our heads.

"The Office Playlist Enthusiast" – a colleague who prided themselves on their impeccable music selection – couldn't resist stepping in to offer song suggestions, leading to a hilarious tug-of-war between the DJ's unconventional choices and The Office Playlist Enthusiast's retro classics.

Amidst the musical mayhem, "The Office Dance-Off Champion" – a colleague with impressive dance moves – took to the floor and attempted to unite the crowd with a series of dance challenges. But it seemed that everyone had their own interpretation of retro dance styles, leading to a chaotic yet uproarious dance-off that left us all in stitches.

"The Office Chef" – a colleague known for their culinary prowess – had prepared a feast fit for a king. The buffet table was a sight to behold, laden with retro-inspired dishes that harkened back to the days of yore.

But even The Office Chef couldn't escape The Comedy of Errors unscathed. As we gathered around the buffet, "The Office Food Critic" – a colleague who always had a way with words – couldn't resist offering their "expert" opinion on each dish.

"Ah, I see you went for the 'Ambitious Aspic Salad.' A bold choice indeed," The Office Food Critic declared, raising an eyebrow.

"The Office Chef" chuckled and played along, introducing the dishes with a flair that only added to the amusement.

As the night wore on, The Office Party took on a life of its own, with each passing moment becoming increasingly absurd and unforgettable.

"The Office Karaoke Diva" – a colleague known for their impressive vocal range – took to the stage and belted out classic ballads and power anthems. The crowd cheered and joined in, creating a raucous sing-along that transformed the party into a makeshift karaoke extravaganza.

But just as we thought The Comedy of Errors had reached its peak, "The Office Prankster" made a grand entrance, clad in a neon suit that glowed in the dark. With a sly grin, they revealed their latest prank – a series of quirky retro-themed photo props that had us striking hilarious poses for the camera.

"The Office Prankster" couldn't resist photobombing every picture, leaving us with a collection of snapshots that captured the sheer joy and absurdity of The Office Party.

As the night drew to a close, The Office Party had become a treasure trove of side-splitting memories. It was a celebration of laughter, camaraderie, and the shared experience of embracing the hilarity that came with being part of an office family.

And so, as we bid farewell to The Office Party, we did so with smiles on our faces and a heart full of gratitude for the moments of pure joy and camaraderie that had enriched our office journey.

For in the end, it wasn't just The Party Planner Extraordinaire's meticulous planning or The Office Chef's culinary delights that made The Office Party memorable, but the comedy of errors and shared laughter that had transformed the event into a truly unforgettable experience.

And so, armed with a renewed sense of camaraderie and a shared treasure trove of comedic memories, we ventured forth into the ever-quirky world of the office, ready to face whatever hilarity and camaraderie the future had in store for us.

For in the end, it was the laughter and camaraderie that made the office not just a place of work, but a place of connection, joy, and unforgettable memories. And armed with humour and unity, we knew that we could conquer any comedy of errors that came our way, turning each mishap into a shared adventure filled with laughter and camaraderie.

The Art of Navigating Office Politics
with a Smile

In the labyrinth of the office, where politics and paperwork intertwined, there resided an enigmatic art form – The Art of Navigating Office Politics. It was a dance of diplomacy, a symphony of tact, and a comedy of wits that required finesse, humour, and a dash of charm. As we delved into the secrets of this art, we found that the key to success was not just survival but navigating with a smile.

"The Office Diplomat" – a colleague renowned for their ability to navigate even the trickiest of political waters – graciously agreed to impart their wisdom on the art of office politics. With a smile that never wavered, they shared their first rule of thumb.

"Always remember, a smile is your secret weapon," The Office Diplomat advised. "It disarms adversaries, puts colleagues at ease, and adds a touch of charm to every interaction."

Armed with this invaluable advice, we ventured forth to conquer the office political landscape. And so, our journey into The Art of Navigating Office Politics with a Smile began.

The first test of our newfound artistry came in the form of "The Cubicle Conundrum" – a situation where coveted office space was up for grabs. As tensions ran high and colleagues vied for the best spots, we approached the situation armed with smiles and a sprinkle of humour.

"The Office Space Negotiator" – a colleague known for their persuasive skills – stepped in to mediate the conundrum. With a smile that could charm the birds from the trees, they facilitated a light-hearted game of "Office Musical Chairs."

As the music played, we gracefully circled the available spaces, each of us moving from one desk to another with a smile. The tension melted away, replaced by laughter and camaraderie.

In the end, we each settled into our new spaces, content with the outcome and grateful for the light-hearted approach that had turned a potential conflict into a shared adventure.

But The Art of Navigating Office Politics with a Smile wasn't just about defusing tensions. It was also about building alliances and forming connections.

"The Office Connector" – a colleague with an uncanny ability to bring people together – demonstrated this art beautifully. With a genuine smile and a knack for finding common ground, they forged alliances between departments, turning once distant colleagues into valuable allies.

"The Office Connector" hosted regular "Coffee Break Mixers," inviting colleagues from different teams to gather for casual conversations over a cup of joe. As we exchanged stories and discovered shared interests, we couldn't help but feel a sense of unity that transcended office politics.

And it wasn't just within the office walls that The Art of Navigating Office Politics with a Smile thrived. It extended to external encounters as well.

"The Client Charmer" – a colleague known for their charisma – taught us the importance of using a smile to build rapport with clients and external partners.

With a smile that could light up a room, "The Client Charmer" effortlessly put clients at ease, turning business meetings into pleasant exchanges that felt more like friendly conversations.

As we observed "The Client Charmer" in action, we learned that a genuine smile could be the key to forging lasting relationships and fostering a sense of trust and camaraderie.

But perhaps the most amusing aspect of The Art of Navigating Office Politics with a Smile was the occasional encounter with "The Office Ego."

"The Office Ego" – a colleague with an inflated sense of self-importance – always seemed to be at the centre of office politics. They had a habit of taking credit for others' ideas and using their smile to charm their way out of any situation.

But little did they know that The Office Ego was no match for The Art of Navigating Office Politics with a Smile. "The Office Mastermind" – a colleague with a keen wit – had a clever strategy for dealing with The Office Ego's antics.

With a smile that concealed a touch of mischief, "The Office Mastermind" crafted a series of subtle pranks that gently exposed The Office Ego's grandiose claims.

During a team meeting, "The Office Mastermind" innocently remarked, "You know, I was just thinking about that brilliant idea you had last week, and it's so similar to the one we discussed last month. It's amazing how ideas seem to circle back, isn't it?"

The Office Ego, caught off guard, could do nothing but chuckle nervously, realizing that their facade had been cracked.

As we witnessed The Office Ego's response, we learned that humour and a smile could be powerful tools for dealing with office politics. It was a way of gently deflating egos and reminding ourselves not to take ourselves too seriously.

And so, as we continued our journey through The Art of Navigating Office Politics with a Smile, we realized that it was more than just a survival tactic — it was a way of infusing our office culture with positivity, camaraderie, and the joy of shared experiences.

"The Office Motivator" — a colleague known for their uplifting pep talks — summed it up perfectly. "A smile is infectious," they declared, their smile radiating warmth. "When we navigate office politics with a smile, we create a positive ripple effect that can transform the entire office environment."

And so, armed with smiles and a touch of humour, we ventured forth into the ever-quirky world of office politics, ready to face whatever challenges and comedic encounters awaited us.

For in the end, it wasn't just about navigating the political landscape but about doing so with a smile that brought joy, unity, and a touch of light-heartedness to the daily dance of office life. And with The Art of Navigating Office Politics with a Smile as our guide, we knew that we could conquer any challenge that came our way, turning each moment into a shared adventure filled with laughter, camaraderie, and the artistry of diplomacy.

The Art of Navigating Office Politics with a Smile

In the labyrinth of the office, where politics and paperwork intertwined, there resided an enigmatic art form – The Art of Navigating Office Politics. It was a dance of diplomacy, a symphony of tact, and a comedy of wits that required finesse, humour, and a dash of charm. As we delved into the secrets of this art, we found that the key to success was not just survival but navigating with a smile.

"The Office Diplomat" – a colleague renowned for their ability to navigate even the trickiest of political waters – graciously agreed to impart their wisdom on the art of office politics. With a smile that never wavered, they shared their first rule of thumb.

"Always remember, a smile is your secret weapon," The Office Diplomat advised. "It disarms adversaries, puts colleagues at ease, and adds a touch of charm to every interaction."

Armed with this invaluable advice, we ventured forth to conquer the office political landscape. And so, our journey into The Art of Navigating Office Politics with a Smile began.

The first test of our newfound artistry came in the form of "The Cubicle Conundrum" – a situation where coveted office space was up for grabs. As tensions ran high and colleagues vied for the best spots, we approached the situation armed with smiles and a sprinkle of humour.

"The Office Space Negotiator" – a colleague known for their persuasive skills – stepped in to mediate the conundrum. With a smile that could charm the birds from the trees, they facilitated a light-hearted game of "Office Musical Chairs."

As the music played, we gracefully circled the available spaces, each of us moving from one desk to another with a smile. The tension melted away, replaced by laughter and camaraderie.

In the end, we each settled into our new spaces, content with the outcome and grateful for the light-hearted approach that had turned a potential conflict into a shared adventure.

But The Art of Navigating Office Politics with a Smile wasn't just about defusing tensions. It was also about building alliances and forming connections.

"The Office Connector" – a colleague with an uncanny ability to bring people together – demonstrated this art beautifully. With a genuine smile and a knack for finding common ground, they forged alliances between departments, turning once distant colleagues into valuable allies.

"The Office Connector" hosted regular "Coffee Break Mixers," inviting colleagues from different teams to gather for casual conversations over a cup of joe. As we exchanged stories and discovered shared interests, we couldn't help but feel a sense of unity that transcended office politics.

And it wasn't just within the office walls that The Art of Navigating Office Politics with a Smile thrived. It extended to external encounters as well.

"The Client Charmer" – a colleague known for their charisma – taught us the importance of using a smile to build rapport with clients and external partners.

With a smile that could light up a room, "The Client Charmer" effortlessly put clients at ease, turning business meetings into pleasant exchanges that felt more like friendly conversations.

As we observed "The Client Charmer" in action, we learned that a genuine smile could be the key to forging lasting relationships and fostering a sense of trust and camaraderie.

But perhaps the most amusing aspect of The Art of Navigating Office Politics with a Smile was the occasional encounter with "The Office Ego."

"The Office Ego" – a colleague with an inflated sense of self-importance – always seemed to be at the centre of office politics. They had a habit of taking credit for others' ideas and using their smile to charm their way out of any situation.

But little did they know that The Office Ego was no match for The Art of Navigating Office Politics with a Smile. "The Office Mastermind" – a colleague with a keen wit – had a clever strategy for dealing with The Office Ego's antics.

With a smile that concealed a touch of mischief, "The Office Mastermind" crafted a series of subtle pranks that gently exposed The Office Ego's grandiose claims.

During a team meeting, "The Office Mastermind" innocently remarked, "You know, I was just thinking about that brilliant idea you had last week, and it's so similar to the one we discussed last month. It's amazing how ideas seem to circle back, isn't it?"

The Office Ego, caught off guard, could do nothing but chuckle nervously, realizing that their facade had been cracked.

As we witnessed The Office Ego's response, we learned that humour and a smile could be powerful tools for dealing with office politics. It was a way of gently deflating egos and reminding ourselves not to take ourselves too seriously.

And so, as we continued our journey through The Art of Navigating Office Politics with a Smile, we realized that it was more than just a survival tactic – it was a way of infusing our office culture with positivity, camaraderie, and the joy of shared experiences.

"The Office Motivator" – a colleague known for their uplifting pep talks – summed it up perfectly. "A smile is infectious," they declared, their smile radiating warmth. "When we navigate office politics with a smile, we create a positive ripple effect that can transform the entire office environment."

And so, armed with smiles and a touch of humour, we ventured forth into the ever-quirky world of office politics, ready to face whatever challenges and comedic encounters awaited us.

For in the end, it wasn't just about navigating the political landscape but about doing so with a smile that brought joy, unity, and a touch of light-heartedness to the daily dance of office life. And with The Art of Navigating Office Politics with a Smile as our guide, we knew that we could conquer any challenge that came our way, turning each moment into a shared adventure filled with laughter, camaraderie, and the artistry of diplomacy.

The Perils of Desk Decorations

In the bustling landscape of the office, where cubicles stood as personalized fortresses and desks became a canvas for self-expression, there lay a perilous endeavour – Desk Decorations. For many, adorning their workspace with quirky decor was a way to infuse a touch of personality into the otherwise mundane environment. But little did we know that this seemingly innocent act could lead to a series of comedic misadventures that would forever be etched into the annals of office lore.

It all began innocently enough, with a wave of creativity sweeping through the office. Colleagues embarked on a mission to transform their desks into miniature worlds of wonder. "The Office Artist" – a colleague with a flair for artistic endeavours – adorned their desk with hand-drawn cartoons and whimsical characters, turning their workspace into a delightful comic strip.

Inspired by The Office Artist's creativity, I decided to unleash my inner decorator. Armed with an assortment of colourful post-it notes, sticky tape, and an abundance of enthusiasm, I set out to give my desk a makeover that would make even the most avant-garde art installations blush.

And so, with determination in my heart and a vision in my mind, I began the perilous journey of Desk Decorations.

The first step was to create a majestic post-it note rainbow that arched gracefully over my computer monitor. With each sticky note meticulously placed, I marvelled at the rainbow taking shape before my eyes.

But little did I know that my ambitious endeavour would soon attract the attention of "The Office Practical Joker" – a colleague known for their mischievous ways. As I stepped away to grab more post-it notes, The Office Practical Joker seized the opportunity to add their artistic touch.

Upon my return, I gasped in shock and laughter as I beheld the work of The Office Practical Joker – a post-it note unicorn with googly eyes and a rainbow-colored mane, playfully prancing amidst my desk decorations.

"Well played, dear joker. Well played," I chuckled, deciding to embrace the unexpected addition to my artistic creation.

But the perils of Desk Decorations didn't end there. As the days went by, my desk became a beacon of eccentricity in the office, drawing curious glances and amused chuckles from passing colleagues.

"The Office Organizer" – a colleague with a penchant for orderliness – eyed my colourful chaos with a mix of bemusement and concern.

"Are you sure you can find anything amidst this post-it note jungle?" The Office Organizer quipped, raising an eyebrow.

I assured them that I had a system in place, albeit a whimsical and color-coded one.

But the true peril of Desk Decorations revealed itself when "The Office Enforcer" – a colleague known for their adherence to office rules and regulations – paid a surprise visit.

"The Office Enforcer" peered at my desk decorations with an unyielding stare, their expression a mix of disbelief and disapproval.

"Are these decorations in compliance with the office decor policy?" The Office Enforcer asked sternly.

I stammered, realizing that I hadn't consulted the office guidelines on desk decorations before embarking on my artistic venture.

"Well, you see, they're all just post-it notes," I offered, trying to defend my colourful creation.

To my relief, "The Office Comedian" intervened with a witty remark. "I believe these decorations fall under the category of 'abstract art meets office supplies.' A true masterpiece!"

The Office Comedian's comment diffused the tension, and "The Office Enforcer" reluctantly retreated, though not without a warning to "maintain a sense of professionalism" amidst my artistic endeavours.

As I navigated the perils of Desk Decorations, I realized that the office had become a battleground of creativity and humour, each desk competing for the title of "most eccentric workspace."

"The Office Minimalist" – a colleague who believed in the power of simplicity – kept their desk free of any decorations, preferring a clean and clutter-free workspace.

"The Office Garden Enthusiast" – a colleague with a green thumb – transformed their desk into a mini oasis, complete with potted plants and miniature garden gnomes.

And then there was "The Office Tech Wizard" – a colleague with a passion for gadgets – whose desk resembled a high-tech command centre, brimming with screens and innovative devices.

But amidst the friendly rivalry and laughter, a new peril arose – "The Office Decoration Thief." This mysterious character had a penchant for playfully "borrowing" items from colleagues' desk decorations and leaving behind cryptic ransom notes.

One day, I returned to my desk to find my post-it note rainbow missing a colour. In its place was a ransom note that read, "For the safe return of the missing hue, leave a bag of gummy bears in the break room."

"The Office Detective" – a colleague with a talent for solving office mysteries – was determined to uncover the identity of The Office Decoration Thief. With a smile and a twinkle in their eye, they set out on a comedic investigation that involved covert surveillance and creative bait.

As the hunt for The Office Decoration Thief continued, I couldn't help but feel a sense of camaraderie with my colleagues. We were bound together by a shared sense of humour and a willingness to embrace the perils and joys of Desk Decorations.

And so, as the chapter of Desk Decorations unfolded, I did so with a smile on my face and a heart full of laughter. It was a tale of creativity, camaraderie, and the art of finding humour in the everyday adventures of office life.

For in the end, it wasn't just about post-it note rainbows or whimsical unicorns, but about the shared experience of navigating the perils of Desk Decorations with a sense of humour and a touch of artistic flair.

And so, armed with a newfound appreciation for the art of Desk Decorations, I ventured forth into the ever-quirky world of the office, ready to face whatever creative misadventures and camaraderie the future had in store for me.

For in the end, it was the laughter and camaraderie that made the office not just a place of work, but a place of connection, joy, and unforgettable memories. And armed with humour and unity, I knew that I could conquer any perils that came my way, turning each moment into a shared adventure

filled with laughter, camaraderie, and the artistry of
desk decorations.

Work-Life Balance

A Myth or a Mirage?

In the bustling landscape of modern work culture, where time seemed to slip through our fingers like sand, there lay a mysterious quest that eluded many – the pursuit of Work-Life Balance. Was it a mythical ideal, forever beyond our reach? Or was it a mirage, an illusion that shimmered tantalizingly on the horizon but vanished as we got closer? This chapter chronicles my comedic odyssey in search of the elusive Work-Life Balance, a journey that was filled with laughter, mishaps, and unexpected discoveries.

The quest for Work-Life Balance began with the best of intentions. Determined to achieve harmony between my professional and personal life, I set out on a quest worthy of a hero in an epic tale. Armed with time management strategies, productivity apps, and a resolute spirit, I embarked on my adventure.

But little did I know that the path to Work-Life Balance was a treacherous one, filled with unforeseen obstacles and comedic twists.

The first challenge I encountered was "The Office Time Thief" – a sneaky creature that seemed determined to steal away every precious minute of my day. From unscheduled meetings to never-ending email chains, The Office Time Thief was relentless in its pursuit of my time.

With a weary sigh, I attempted to fend off The Office Time Thief's advances, employing time management techniques that promised to maximize productivity.

"The Office Time Keeper" – a colleague known for their punctuality – offered to be my ally in the battle against The Office Time Thief. Armed with an alarm clock and an unwavering commitment to sticking to schedules, The Office Time Keeper attempted to keep me on track.

But as The Office Time Thief continued to lay traps for me, I found myself caught in a never-ending cycle of work-related tasks. The mirage of Work-Life Balance seemed to drift further away, leaving me feeling like a hamster on a never-ending wheel of productivity.

As the days turned into weeks, I began to wonder if Work-Life Balance was merely a myth – a tantalizing ideal that was forever out of reach. But then, a ray of hope appeared on the horizon.

"The Office Zen Master" – a colleague known for their calm demeanour and ability to find balance amidst chaos – offered their wisdom.

"Work-Life Balance is not a destination to be reached but a journey to be embraced," The Office Zen Master said, their serene smile giving me a glimmer of hope.

With their guidance, I learned that perhaps the mirage of Work-Life Balance was not a fixed destination but a shifting landscape that required constant recalibration.

And so, armed with a newfound perspective, I ventured forth once again in pursuit of Work-Life Balance. This time, I embraced flexibility and humour, allowing myself to bend and adapt to the ebb and flow of work and life.

But just as I thought I was making progress, a new challenge emerged — "The Office Overachiever." This mythical creature had an uncanny ability to take on more work than seemed humanly possible, leaving the rest of us in awe and exhaustion.

With their boundless energy and perpetual smile, The Office Overachiever seemed to defy the laws of time and space.

"I've found the secret to Work-Life Balance — more work!" The Office Overachiever declared with a wink.

As I observed The Office Overachiever in action, I couldn't help but wonder if they had discovered a hidden loophole in the quest for Work-Life Balance. But deep down, I knew that their approach was not sustainable.

And so, armed with a dose of reality and a touch of humour, I continued on my quest, determined to find a balance that was right for me.

As the chapters of my comedic odyssey unfolded, I discovered unexpected allies in my pursuit of Work-Life Balance.

"The Office Humourist" — a colleague with an arsenal of jokes and witty remarks — taught me the importance of finding humour in the everyday challenges of balancing work and life.

"The Office Cheerleader" — a colleague known for their enthusiastic pep talks — lifted my spirits during moments of frustration and exhaustion.

"The Office Empathizer" — a colleague with a talent for understanding others' emotions — offered a listening ear and a reassuring pat on the back during moments of doubt.

Together, we embarked on a shared adventure in search of Work-Life Balance, armed with laughter, camaraderie, and a dash of mischief.

And then, in a moment of unexpected clarity, I realized that perhaps Work-Life Balance was not a destination at all, but a state of mind.

It was about finding joy and fulfilment in both work and life, and embracing the imperfections and unexpected detours along the way.

"The Office Philosopher" — a colleague known for their contemplative musings — summed it up perfectly.

"Work-Life Balance is not about rigidly dividing our time between work and life," The Office Philosopher mused. "It's about finding harmony and meaning in all aspects of our journey."

With this newfound wisdom, I finally understood that Work-Life Balance was not a myth or a mirage, but a quest that required a willingness to adapt, a sense of humour, and a supportive community of colleagues.

As the chapter of my comedic odyssey came to a close, I did so with a smile on my face and a heart full of laughter. It had been a journey of self-discovery, camaraderie, and the art of finding balance in the midst of life's chaos.

For in the end, it wasn't just about achieving the elusive Work-Life Balance, but about embracing the journey with all its mishaps and triumphs, and finding joy in the shared adventure of work and life.

And so, armed with humour and unity, I ventured forth into the ever-quirky world of work-life balance, ready to face whatever comedic misadventures and camaraderie the future had in store for me.

For in the end, it was the laughter and camaraderie that made the office not just a place of work, but a place of connection, joy, and unforgettable memories. And armed with humour and unity, I knew that I could navigate the quest for work-life balance, turning each moment into a shared adventure filled with laughter, camaraderie, and the artistry of finding harmony amidst life's unpredictable journey.

The Day I Learned About "Reply Hazy, Try Again"

In the bustling realm of the office, where deadlines loomed like storm clouds and emails poured in like a relentless downpour, there existed a mystical oracle – the "Magic 8 Ball." Though officially a toy, the Magic 8 Ball had become an informal advisor to those seeking answers to life's pressing questions. And so, it came to pass that on one fateful day, I discovered the power – and hilarity – of the Magic 8 Ball's enigmatic response, "Reply Hazy, Try Again."

The journey into the world of the Magic 8 Ball began innocently enough, with "The Office Oracle" – a colleague known for their uncanny ability to predict future office trends – introducing me to the mystical toy.

"Ask a question, shake the ball, and await the answer," The Office Oracle explained with a mysterious smile.

Intrigued, I decided to put the Magic 8 Ball to the test. Holding it with reverence, I posed my first question, "Will I meet the deadline for the Johnson project?"

With a hopeful heart, I shook the Magic 8 Ball and turned it over, waiting for its sage wisdom to be revealed.

"Reply Hazy, Try Again," the Magic 8 Ball declared, its cryptic response eliciting laughter from The Office Oracle.

"Well, that's not exactly a reassuring answer," I chuckled, feeling a mix of amusement and bewilderment.

But little did I know that my encounter with the Magic 8 Ball had only just begun. Throughout the day, I found myself turning to the mystical oracle for guidance on various office dilemmas.

"Will the boss approve my proposal?" I asked, giving the Magic 8 Ball a vigorous shake.

"Cannot predict now," it replied, leaving me with a sense of uncertainty that matched its enigmatic response.

And so, the day passed in a flurry of questions and whimsical answers from the Magic 8 Ball.

"Should I go for a coffee break now?" I inquired.

"Ask again later," the Magic 8 Ball replied, prompting a chuckle from The Office Oracle.

As the day wore on, my colleagues caught wind of my fascination with the Magic 8 Ball, and soon, it became a communal source of amusement and playful guidance.

"The Office Dreamer" – a colleague known for their imaginative ideas – posed the question, "Will my new project proposal revolutionize the industry?"

The Magic 8 Ball's response was classic, "Outlook not so good," sending us into fits of laughter.

"The Office Optimist" – a colleague with an unwavering positive outlook – asked, "Will our team exceed the sales targets this quarter?"

The Magic 8 Ball's answer was characteristically mysterious, "Ask again later."

And so, the day continued with a whimsical dance of questions and enigmatic answers from the Magic 8 Ball, transforming the office into a light-hearted playground of laughter and camaraderie.

But then, just as the novelty of the Magic 8 Ball seemed to wear off, a moment of unexpected wisdom emerged.

"The Office Confidante" – a colleague known for their genuine empathy – asked, "Will everything be okay?"

I hesitated, unsure if the Magic 8 Ball could provide solace in moments of uncertainty.

But as I turned the Magic 8 Ball over, its response was surprisingly profound – "Focus on the present moment."

"The Office Confidante" smiled, their eyes filled with understanding.

"It's true," they said softly. "Sometimes, we get so caught up in seeking answers that we forget to be present and focus on what we can control."

Their words resonated deeply, and I realized that the Magic 8 Ball's enigmatic answers had a peculiar way of teaching valuable lessons amidst the comedy and laughter.

As the day drew to a close, I bid farewell to the Magic 8 Ball, grateful for the light-hearted adventure it had brought to the office.

But the magic of the Magic 8 Ball didn't end there. In the days that followed, I found myself heeding its advice to "Reply Hazy, Try Again" in moments of uncertainty and seeking solace in its reminder to "Focus on the present moment."

"The Office Visionary" – a colleague known for their insightful wisdom – offered a parting reflection on the experience.

"The Magic 8 Ball may seem like a playful toy, but perhaps its true magic lies in its ability to remind us of the unpredictability of life," The Office Visionary mused. "It's a reminder that sometimes, we don't need all the answers, and that's okay. Embrace the uncertainty and find joy in the journey."

And so, armed with a touch of whimsy and a newfound appreciation for the magic of the present moment, I ventured forth into the ever-quirky world of the office, ready to face whatever comedic misadventures and camaraderie the future had in store for me.

For in the end, it was the laughter and camaraderie that made the office not just a place of work, but a place of connection, joy, and unforgettable memories. And armed with humour and unity, I knew that I could navigate the mysterious path of the Magic 8 Ball, turning each moment into a shared adventure filled with laughter, camaraderie, and the artistry of embracing the magic of the present moment.

The Great Bathroom Break Debate

In the labyrinth of the office, where deadlines loomed large and productivity reigned supreme, there existed an age-old dilemma – The Great Bathroom Break Debate. For many, the quest to answer the pressing question of when and how long a bathroom break should be was a comedic odyssey filled with awkward encounters, hilarious mishaps, and unexpected wisdom.

It all began innocently enough, with the unspoken understanding that bathroom breaks were a necessity, a natural part of being human. But as days turned into weeks, and weeks into months, a subtle tension began to simmer beneath the surface.

"The Office Efficiency Guru" – a colleague known for their unwavering dedication to maximizing productivity – raised an eyebrow during a team meeting.

"I've noticed a slight decrease in productivity lately," The Office Efficiency Guru remarked, their gaze lingering on their watch.

The unspoken message was clear – bathroom breaks were eating away at precious work hours.

"The Office Clock Watcher" – a colleague with a keen eye for punctuality – joined in with a nod of agreement.

"I've calculated that if we each spend just one extra minute in the bathroom per day, it adds up to hours of lost productivity over the course of a year," The Office Clock Watcher declared with a hint of concern.

And so, The Great Bathroom Break Debate was born, igniting a comedic battle of wills and a quest to find the perfect balance between bathroom breaks and productivity.

"The Office Rulemaker" – a colleague known for their love of guidelines and regulations – proposed a strict bathroom break schedule.

"We shall take a five-minute bathroom break at precisely 10:00 AM and a ten-minute break at 2:00 PM. No exceptions," The Office Rulemaker declared, their pen poised to draft the official decree.

But their proposal was met with resistance. "The Office Rebel" – a colleague with a mischievous streak – rolled their eyes and quipped, "We're not in boot camp; we're in an office!"

"The Office Free Spirit" – a colleague known for their carefree attitude – chimed in with a playful grin.

"Why not let us listen to the call of nature when it beckons? We're adults, after all," The Office Free Spirit suggested, garnering nods of agreement from some and sceptical glances from others.

And so, the debate raged on, with each side presenting compelling arguments in the quest for the perfect bathroom break balance.

But amidst the comedic clash of ideas, a voice of reason emerged – "The Office Sage" – a colleague known for their wise insights and ability to find harmony amidst chaos.

"The key is flexibility," The Office Sage proposed with a knowing smile. "Let each individual determine their bathroom break needs, and trust that they will prioritize their work responsibilities."

"The Office Mediator" – a colleague with a talent for resolving conflicts – added, "It's about finding a balance that works for everyone. After all, we're a team."

And so, a compromise was reached. The Office agreed to allow flexibility in bathroom breaks, with the understanding that everyone would prioritize their responsibilities and be mindful of their time.

As the days went by, a newfound sense of camaraderie and humour emerged around The Great Bathroom Break Debate.

"The Office Hydration Advocate" – a colleague with a passion for wellness – suggested that more bathroom breaks might actually promote better health and hydration.

"Let's embrace the concept of 'productive breaks'," The Office Hydration Advocate declared. "A quick walk to the restroom can also be a moment to stretch and refresh our minds!"

"The Office Storyteller" – a colleague known for their captivating narratives – shared a hilarious tale of a bathroom break gone wrong, complete with a stuck stall door and a heroic janitor who came to the rescue.

The tale had us all in stitches, and we realized that perhaps The Great Bathroom Break Debate was not just about productivity but also about finding moments of laughter and connection amidst the daily grind.

And then, a moment of unexpected wisdom came from "The Office Parent" – a colleague known for their balancing act of work and family responsibilities.

"Sometimes, we need a few extra minutes in the restroom to catch our breath and regroup," The Office Parent shared. "It's about respecting each other's needs and understanding that life happens."

With this newfound wisdom, The Great Bathroom Break Debate transformed from a source of tension into a shared adventure of camaraderie and understanding.

"The Office Connector" – a colleague known for their ability to bring people together – proposed a playful solution.

"Let's turn our bathroom breaks into moments of connection. Instead of avoiding eye contact in the restroom, let's take a moment to greet each other and share a smile," The Office Connector suggested.

And so, The Great Bathroom Break Debate took a surprising turn, with restroom encounters becoming moments of camaraderie and laughter.

"The Office Jokester" – a colleague known for their quick wit – took it a step further by placing a joke-of-the-day on the restroom door, turning each bathroom visit into a moment of levity.

As the chapter of The Great Bathroom Break Debate came to a close, I realized that it wasn't just about finding the perfect bathroom break balance, but about embracing the humour and camaraderie that came with the journey.

For in the end, it was the laughter and understanding that made the office not just a place of work, but a place of connection, joy, and unforgettable memories.

And armed with humour and unity, I knew that I could navigate The Great Bathroom Break Debate and the ever-quirky world of the office, turning each moment into a shared adventure filled with laughter, camaraderie, and the artistry of finding balance in the midst of life's comedic escapades.

The Office Fashion Faux Pas

In the vibrant realm of the office, where business attire mingled with personal style, there existed a peculiar phenomenon – The Office Fashion Faux Pas. For many, the quest to dress professionally while expressing individuality was a comedic tightrope walk filled with fashion mishaps, humorous encounters, and valuable lessons in the art of office dressing.

It all began innocently enough, with each of us trying to strike the perfect balance between looking professional and showcasing our unique personalities. But little did we know that the office fashion landscape was a minefield of potential faux pas, waiting to be discovered.

My own misadventure in the realm of office fashion began on a bright Monday morning when I decided to showcase my love for bold patterns. Armed with confidence, I donned a vibrant polka-dot shirt that exuded cheerful energy.

As I stepped into the office, I felt like a fashion-forward trailblazer, ready to embrace the week with panache.

But my moment of fashion triumph was short-lived.

"The Office Fashionista" – a colleague known for their impeccable style – took one look at my polka-dot ensemble and raised an eyebrow.

"Channelling your inner avant-garde artist today, are we?" The Office Fashionista quipped, their perfectly styled hair and chic outfit contrasting with my bold choice.

Unfazed, I took The Office Fashionista's comment in stride, dismissing it as a matter of personal taste.

But little did I know that The Office Fashion Faux Pas had only just begun.

"The Office Minimalist" – a colleague known for their clean and streamlined fashion choices – raised an amused eyebrow during a team meeting.

"Going for the eclectic look today?" The Office Minimalist remarked, their subtle hint of sarcasm eliciting chuckles from others.

Undeterred, I continued to experiment with my fashion choices, embracing the playful side of office dressing.

"The Office Accessory Guru" – a colleague known for their penchant for bold accessories – encouraged my fashion exploration.

"Own it! Fashion is about self-expression, after all," The Office Accessory Guru declared with a reassuring smile.

Buoyed by The Office Accessory Guru's support, I decided to take my office fashion game to the next level.

"The Office Trendsetter" – a colleague known for their ability to set fashion trends – was my inspiration. With their confident stride and effortless style, The Office Trendsetter seemed to effortlessly navigate the world of office fashion.

Determined to follow in their fashionable footsteps, I stepped into the office one day wearing an outfit that could only be described as "fashion-forward experimental."

A combination of bold prints, mismatched colours, and a hint of retro flair, my outfit made a statement – though perhaps not the one I intended.

As I made my way through the office, I noticed curious glances and amused smiles. It seemed that my fashion-forward experiment had caught the attention of The Office Trendsetter.

"Embracing the cutting-edge, are we?" The Office Trendsetter remarked, their eyes twinkling with amusement.

With a sheepish grin, I acknowledged my fashion folly, realizing that perhaps some fashion risks were best left to the experts.

But amidst the comedic misadventures in the realm of office fashion, valuable lessons began to emerge.

"The Office Classic" – a colleague known for their timeless and elegant style – offered a piece of fashion wisdom.

"Office dressing doesn't have to be a high-stakes runway show. A classic and polished look never goes out of style," The Office Classic advised with a touch of grace.

"The Office Comfort Connoisseur" – a colleague known for their practical yet stylish fashion choices – shared their insight.

"It's all about finding fashion pieces that make you feel confident and comfortable," The Office Comfort Connoisseur explained. "If you feel good in what you're wearing, it will show."

With these words in mind, I began to embrace a more balanced approach to office fashion, blending classic elegance with playful touches that reflected my personality.

"The Office Mix-and-Matcher" – a colleague known for their creativity in mixing and matching fashion pieces – became my mentor in the art of office dressing.

"Experiment with different combinations and find your own unique style," The Office Mix-and-Matcher encouraged. "Fashion is about expressing who you are."

Armed with newfound fashion wisdom, I navigated the world of office fashion with a touch of humour and a dash of self-assuredness.

And as the chapter of The Office Fashion Faux Pas came to a close, I did so with a smile on my face and a heart full of laughter. It had been a journey of fashion exploration, camaraderie, and the art of finding confidence in the choices we make.

For in the end, it wasn't just about avoiding fashion faux pas, but about embracing our individuality and finding joy in the comedic adventures of office dressing.

And so, armed with humour and unity, I ventured forth into the ever-quirky world of office fashion, ready to face whatever misadventures and camaraderie the future had in store for me.

For in the end, it was the laughter and camaraderie that made the office not just a place of work, but a place of connection, joy, and unforgettable memories. And armed with humour and unity, I knew that I could navigate the comedic terrain of office fashion, turning each moment into a shared adventure filled with laughter, camaraderie, and the artistry of expressing ourselves through fashion.

The Case of the Mysterious Office Ghost

In the labyrinth of the office, where whispers of deadlines and echoes of keyboard clicks filled the air, there was a mystery that defied explanation – The Case of the Mysterious Office Ghost. For many, the ghostly presence was a comedic enigma, leaving behind a trail of baffling occurrences and sparking the curiosity of even the most sceptical minds.

It all began on a stormy Monday morning when "The Office Sceptic" – a colleague known for their scepticism and logic – arrived at their desk to find their stapler mysteriously perched on top of their computer monitor.

"Hmm, must be a prank," The Office Sceptic muttered, dismissing the incident as a playful office trick.

But as days turned into weeks, and more peculiar events occurred, The Case of the Mysterious Office Ghost became an unsolvable puzzle that captivated the entire office.

Reports of misplaced coffee mugs, mysteriously rearranged office supplies, and flickering lights circulated like wildfire.

"The Office Believer" – a colleague with an open mind and a penchant for the supernatural – proposed the idea of an office ghost.

"Perhaps there's a friendly spirit among us, just having a bit of fun," The Office Believer suggested with a twinkle in their eye.

"The Office Detective" – a colleague known for their investigative skills – took the lead in unravelling the mystery. Armed with a magnifying glass and a keen eye for detail, The Office Detective began collecting clues.

First, they examined security footage, looking for any signs of an intruder. But the footage revealed nothing out of the ordinary – just a normal day at the office.

Next, they interviewed colleagues who had experienced strange occurrences. But each person's account was met with a shrug of confusion and bewilderment.

"It's like the office has a mischievous secret admirer," The Office Detective mused, scratching their head in puzzlement.

As the investigation continued, The Case of the Mysterious Office Ghost became the talk of the office, sparking a mix of excitement and trepidation.

"The Office Storyteller" – a colleague known for their captivating narratives – added fuel to the mystery with their imaginative tales of ghostly encounters.

"I heard the ghost once played a haunting melody on the office piano late at night," The Office Storyteller declared, their eyes wide with wonder.

The tale had us all on the edge of our seats, wondering if there was any truth to the ghostly rumours.

As the days passed, the office became a playground of ghostly humour and camaraderie. Colleagues playfully blamed the ghost for misplaced items, and "The Office Prankster" – a colleague known for their mischievous ways – began leaving ghost-themed surprises on colleagues' desks.

One morning, "The Office Prankster" set up a trail of ghost footprints leading to The Office Sceptic's desk, prompting laughter and puzzled looks from everyone.

"The Office Sceptic" chuckled, shaking their head in amusement. "Nice try, but I'm not falling for your ghostly tricks."

But little did they know that the ghostly occurrences were about to take an unexpected turn.

"The Office Technophile" – a colleague known for their love of all things tech – proposed setting up surveillance cameras to catch the ghost in action.

With a mix of curiosity and scepticism, we agreed to give it a try. The office transformed into a pseudo-investigation headquarters, with cameras placed strategically throughout the office.

And then, just as we thought The Case of the Mysterious Office Ghost might remain unsolved, the cameras captured something unexpected.

In the dead of night, when the office was deserted and the lights were dimmed, a faint figure appeared on the screen.

"The Office Believer" gasped, their eyes widening in astonishment. "It's the ghost!"

But upon closer inspection, we realized that the mysterious figure was none other than "The Office Night Owl" – a colleague known for working late into the night.

"I guess my late-night work sessions have a ghostly aura," The Office Night Owl chuckled, a hint of mischief in their eyes.

And so, The Case of the Mysterious Office Ghost was solved – not by a supernatural presence but by the presence of a dedicated colleague burning the midnight oil.

The revelation sparked laughter and applause, turning The Case of the Mysterious Office Ghost into a comedic tale of office camaraderie and playful imagination.

"The Office Believer" grinned, not the least bit disappointed that the ghostly mystery had been debunked.

"It may not be a ghost, but it's still a fun and mysterious adventure," The Office Believer declared with a touch of wonder.

As the chapter of The Case of the Mysterious Office Ghost came to a close, I did so with a smile on my face and a heart full of laughter. It had been a journey of comedic investigations, camaraderie, and the art of finding humour in the unexplained.

For in the end, it wasn't just about solving a mystery but about embracing the moments of laughter and connection that made the office not just a place of work, but a place of shared joy and unforgettable memories.

And so, armed with humour and unity, I ventured forth into the ever-quirky world of the office, ready to face whatever comedic misadventures and camaraderie the future had in store for me.

For in the end, it was the laughter and camaraderie that made the office not just a place of work, but a place of connection, joy, and the artistry of finding humour in the mysteries of everyday life. And armed with humour and unity, I knew that I could navigate the comedic terrain of office life, turning each moment into a shared adventure filled with laughter, camaraderie, and the artistry of unravelling the enigmatic wonders of the workplace.

Team-Building Shenanigans

Surviving Trust Falls and More

In the bustling landscape of the office, where work goals loomed large and deadlines pressed like a relentless clock, there lay a peculiar tradition – Team-Building Shenanigans. For many, team-building activities were a comedic odyssey filled with awkward encounters, hilarious mishaps, and unexpected bonds forged amidst the chaos of trust falls and other quirky challenges.

It all began innocently enough with the promise of a day away from our desks, filled with camaraderie and team-building exercises. But little did we know that the day would be a rollercoaster ride of laughter and the art of surviving the unorthodox challenges ahead.

As we gathered in the office meeting room, "The Office Enthusiast" – a colleague known for their infectious enthusiasm – set the tone for the day.

"Get ready for a day of epic team bonding!" The Office Enthusiast declared, their eyes gleaming with excitement.

Our first challenge was the classic "Trust Fall" – a test of faith and teamwork.

"The Office Daredevil" – a colleague known for their bold and adventurous spirit – volunteered to go first. With a deep breath and a leap of faith, The Office

Daredevil fell backward into the waiting arms of the team.

But as we attempted the trust fall one by one, some less-than-graceful landings ensued.

"The Office Stumbler" – a colleague known for their occasional clumsiness – stumbled during their fall, prompting laughter from the team.

"Don't worry; I'm okay!" The Office Stumbler reassured, their good-natured humour diffusing any embarrassment.

And so, the trust fall became a moment of both trust and laughter, setting the tone for the day's adventures.

Next up was the "Human Knot" – a test of patience and problem-solving. We stood in a circle, each person reaching out to hold hands with two others at random. The objective was to untangle ourselves and form a circle without letting go of hands.

"The Office Strategist" – a colleague known for their strategic thinking – took charge.

"Let's approach this systematically," The Office Strategist advised, guiding us through a series of twists and turns.

But as we attempted to untangle ourselves, hilarity ensued. Arms became entangled, and laughter echoed through the room.

"We're in a tangle of arms and chaos!" The Office Jokester quipped, earning a round of chuckles from the team.

As we continued to grapple with the human knot, we found ourselves laughing, bonding, and working together to navigate the comedic labyrinth of limbs.

After surviving the human knot, we embarked on the ultimate team-building challenge – a competitive game of "Office Olympics." From paper airplane contests to "Flip Cup" with water cups, we embraced our inner child and revelled in the joy of playful camaraderie.

"The Office Cheerleader" – a colleague known for their enthusiastic pep talks – cheered us on during each challenge.

"You've got this! Show those paper airplanes who's boss!" The Office Cheerleader encouraged, their infectious energy driving us forward.

"The Office Competitive Spirit" – a colleague known for their competitive edge – jumped into the games with zeal, determined to win each round.

But amidst the competitive spirit, the day's true magic lay in the unexpected connections formed amidst the chaos.

"The Office Listener" – a colleague known for their attentive ear – offered a listening ear and a supportive word during moments of self-doubt.

"Believe in yourself; you've got this!" The Office Listener encouraged, their kindness bolstering our confidence.

"The Office Encourager" – a colleague with a talent for boosting morale – offered words of praise and support to each team member, celebrating even the smallest victories.

"You're all winners in my book!" The Office Encourager declared, their applause fuelling our determination.

And so, as the day of Team-Building Shenanigans came to a close, I did so with a smile on my face and a heart full of laughter. It had been a journey of laughter, camaraderie, and the art of building connections amidst the comedic challenges of trust falls and human knots.

For in the end, it wasn't just about the trust falls and games, but about the shared adventure of navigating the unorthodox challenges of Team-Building Shenanigans and finding joy in the camaraderie that brought us closer together.

As we returned to the office, we carried with us the laughter and memories of a day filled with team-building shenanigans, forging bonds that would last far beyond the day's adventures.

And so, armed with humour and unity, I ventured forth into the ever-quirky world of the office, ready to face whatever comedic misadventures and camaraderie the future had in store for me.

For in the end, it was the laughter and camaraderie that made the office not just a place of work, but a place of connection, joy, and unforgettable memories. And armed with humour and unity, I knew that I could navigate the comedic terrain of office life, turning each moment into a shared adventure filled with laughter, camaraderie, and the artistry of building bonds that would stand the test of time.

Farewell, First Job

Reflecting on the Hilarious Journey

In the realm of the office, where the echoes of keyboard clicks filled the air and the scent of fresh coffee wafted through the halls, a momentous occasion was on the horizon – my farewell from my first job. As I prepared to bid adieu to the place where my career had taken its first steps, I couldn't help but reflect on the hilarious journey that had brought me to this bittersweet moment.

It all began with wide-eyed excitement and nervous anticipation as I walked through the office doors on my first day. Armed with my freshly ironed shirt and a sense of determination, I was ready to conquer the world of work.

But little did I know that my first job would be a comedic playground filled with misadventures and unforgettable moments.

"The Office Mentor" – a seasoned colleague known for their sage advice – took me under their wing.

"Welcome to the office jungle! Get ready for a rollercoaster ride," The Office Mentor declared with a knowing smile.

And so, the rollercoaster ride began with a series of comedic missteps that would have made a veteran office worker chuckle.

First up was the infamous "Office Printer Curse" – a phenomenon that seemed to strike all new employees without fail.

"The Office IT Guru" – a colleague known for their technical prowess – was summoned to rescue me from the clutches of the malfunctioning printer.

"Ah, the printer gremlins strike again," The Office IT Guru remarked, their fingers dancing across the keyboard in a miraculous dance of troubleshooting.

As the printer finally sprang to life, I couldn't help but laugh at the absurdity of my first encounter with the Office Printer Curse.

But it was not just the office technology that provided moments of hilarity; it was the quirky cast of characters that made the office an unpredictable comedy stage.

There was "The Office Comedian" – a colleague known for their quick wit and ability to turn even the most mundane tasks into moments of levity.

"Who's ready for the Monday morning marathon of meetings?" The Office Comedian quipped, eliciting laughter from the team.

And then there was "The Office Storyteller" – a colleague known for their captivating narratives and knack for turning office anecdotes into riveting tales.

"I once spilled coffee on the boss's shirt during a meeting. It was a fashion statement he'd never forget," The Office Storyteller recounted, their eyes twinkling with mischief.

And of course, there was "The Office Foodie" – a colleague known for their love of culinary delights and their enthusiasm for office potlucks.

"Today's potluck theme is international cuisine. Get ready for a global feast!" The Office Foodie announced with delight, igniting excitement for the gastronomic adventure ahead.

As the days turned into weeks and the weeks into months, I found myself navigating the comedic labyrinth of office life with a mix of determination and humour.

There were moments of triumph – landing my first big project and receiving praise from the boss – that filled me with a sense of accomplishment.

But there were also moments of hilarity – like the time I accidentally sent a personal email to the entire office or the day I unknowingly wore mismatched shoes – that reminded me not to take myself too seriously.

"The Office Perfectionist" – a colleague known for their meticulous attention to detail – offered a valuable lesson amidst the comedy.

"Embrace the imperfections; they make life interesting," The Office Perfectionist advised, their wise words sinking in.

And so, armed with a touch of humour and a newfound appreciation for the comedic moments, I continued my journey through the world of work.

But amidst the laughter and camaraderie, a bittersweet realization began to dawn on me – it was time to say farewell to my first job.

As my last day approached, I couldn't help but feel a mix of emotions – gratitude for the opportunities and memories, and a hint of sadness to leave behind the people and the place that had shaped my career.

But in true office fashion, my farewell was not without its comedic moments.

"The Office Memory Keeper" – a colleague known for their knack of preserving memories – surprised me with a scrapbook filled with photos, notes, and funny anecdotes from my time at the office.

"Remember the time we all dressed up as superheroes for Halloween? You made one hilarious Wonder Woman!" The Office Memory Keeper reminisced, and we all laughed at the memory.

"The Office Organizer" – a colleague known for their impeccable planning skills – surprised me with a farewell party complete with decorations and a cake that read, "Farewell, First Job – On to New Adventures!"

As we gathered to bid adieu, I found myself surrounded by laughter, camaraderie, and a sense of appreciation for the comedic journey that had been my first job.

"The Office Visionary" – a colleague known for their forward-thinking perspective – offered a parting reflection.

"Every journey has its twists and turns, but it's the laughter and camaraderie that make the ride worthwhile," The Office Visionary mused. "Embrace the humour, cherish the memories, and step into your next adventure with a heart full of gratitude."

And so, as I bid farewell to my first job with a heart full of gratitude and laughter, I knew that I would carry with me the comedic memories, the camaraderie, and the valuable lessons learned in the vibrant realm of the office.

For in the end, it wasn't just a job; it was a journey of laughter, camaraderie, and the artistry of finding humour in the everyday misadventures of office life.

As I stepped out of the office doors for the last time, I knew that I was not just saying goodbye to a place, but to a chapter filled with comedy, friendship, and unforgettable memories.

Armed with humour and unity, I ventured forth into the ever-quirky world of new adventures, ready to face whatever comedic misadventures and camaraderie the future had in store for me.

For in the end, it was the laughter and camaraderie that made the office not just a place of work, but a place of connection, joy, and the artistry of finding humour in the journey of life. And armed with humour and unity, I knew that I could navigate the comedic terrain of new adventures, turning each moment into a shared adventure filled with laughter, camaraderie, and the artistry of embracing the comedic journey that life had in store.

www.ingramcontent.com/pod-product-compliance
Lightning Source LLC
Chambersburg PA
CBHW070946260726
48661CB00003B/1144